MIKE MENTZER'S COMPLETE BOOK OF WEIGHT TRAINING

MIKE MENTZER'S COMPLETE BOOK OF WEIGHT TRAINING

Mike Mentzer
and
Ardy Friedberg

QUILL

New York • 1983

To my father, Harry Mentzer, who bought my first set of barbells and encouraged me to excel

To Susie, Ruthie, and Eric, with love and thanks for making it all possible

Library of Congress Cataloging in Publication Data

Mentzer, Mike.
  Mike Mentzer's Complete book of weight training.

  Includes index.
  1. Weight lifting.   2. Bodybuilding.
II. Friedberg, Ardy.   II. Title.   III. Title:
Complete book of weight training.
[GV546.M4   1983]   613.7'1   82-18632
ISBN 0-688-00775-9
ISBN 0-688-01600-6 (pbk.)

Printed in the United States of America

First Quill Edition

1 2 3 4 5 6 7 8 9 10

BOOK DESIGN BY FRANK JAMES CANGELOSI

PREFACE

The "Age of Fitness" has settled in and become an accepted part of the American life-style. Men and women, boys and girls are now concerned with their physical condition as never before, and millions of people—possibly as many as ninety million—are actively trying to do something to improve their state of health.

The medical benefits of exercise seem no longer in doubt and the message is being broadcast that indeed, if you exercise regularly, not only your body but also your mind benefits, and that you will feel better and possibly even live longer.

The primary concern of most people who exercise *is* increasing longevity, staving off illness, old age, and above all, avoiding heart attack. Until word got out that running was good for cardiovascular fitness, the few solitary runners weaving their way through the parks and streets were looked on as anomalies at best and freaks at worst. Then suddenly running was discovered to have very beneficial effects on weight, body composition, oxygen uptake, and cardiorespiratory circulation. All of this added up to better health for the regular exerciser.

Today you would have to be an ostrich to be unaware that fitness is a national watchword. People are on the move. The gyms and health clubs are full, there are lines at the tennis courts, and the swimming pools are overflowing with splashing humanity. Everywhere people are talking about health, fitness, diet, exercise. It's much more common to hear talk about split times than stock splits, and not since short skirts have the ankle and knee received so much critical attention.

I think that all of this activity is fantastic but I'm especially pleased that after all these years, weight training has at last assumed its rightful place in the hierarchy of fitness activities. I have known for years that weight training is capable of building much more than muscle mass, and that, properly performed, weight-lifting exercises can allow the exerciser to reach any desired level of strength, power, flexibility, and cardiovascular fitness.

If you are fit you can handle most of life's situations and still have enough left to do things that demand extra energy and exertion with a minimum of fatigue. It also means you can handle stress and make the necessary mental adjustments to conduct the business of daily life and have fun, too.

Muscular strength, the kind you can get only from lifting weights, is a vital component of fitness. Man's very existence depends on his muscles. Body movement is impossible without muscle action, and muscles are vital to other bodily functions. The heart, after all, is a muscle, and digestion, breathing, even elimination are all impossible without muscle contraction. The stronger the muscles the more easily all of these functions are performed.

Weight training is now recognized as one of the most complete and efficient methods of achieving and maintaining physical fitness. *Mike Mentzer's Complete Book of Weight Training* gives you the whole story.

CONTENTS

INTRODUCTION

A 1979 Perrier survey on fitness in America estimated that 4.7 million people train regularly with weights. That's more than the number of skiers or racquetball players. There are probably an equal number of part-time weight lifters who use barbells and dumbbells to supplement their regular form of exercise. This means there may be at least 9 million people out there with at least an interest in, and a rudimentary knowledge of the sport, and this moves weight training ahead of golf, table tennis, and even Frisbee in the hierarchy of exercise.

The New York Times says, "The body of the 80s," for both men and women, will exude strength and dynamism and will display "clearly defined muscles, symmetry, and even some bulk." Fashion dictators like Calvin Klein are emphasizing the well-muscled physique in their new designs. And even Dr. George Sheehan, the runner's philosopher, says, "Weight training may well surpass running and become the training style of the 80s."

Television is devoting a significant amount of time to coverage of Olympic and power-lifting competitions, physique shows, the Mr. Universe and Mr. Olympia contests, to other strength-oriented contests like "The Strongest Man" event, and even men's and women's wrist wrestling. Women's weight-lifting and body-building competitions are also getting their share of coverage. Movies, advertising campaigns, and weekly television shows are featuring body-builders in a variety of roles. The specialized magazines in the field are rapidly increasing circulation, sales of equipment are in the tens of millions of dollars a year, and attendance at weight-lifting events and physique shows is at an all-time high. In short, there is a tremendous amount of public interest and participation in all aspects of the "iron" world.

The boom in weight training in this country (interest has been high in the rest of the world for decades) follows closely on the heels of the physical-fitness craze that has left its craziness behind and become part of the American culture. Men, women, and children, regardless of age, now aspire to the healthy look and the sculptured body. No more is there any reverence for the frail, model look. Contours and strength are in. It should be no surprise, then, that the popularity of weight training for strength and total fitness has skyrocketed.

Today, in basements and Nautilus clubs, in health spas and gyms, in bedrooms and garages, people are "pumping iron" in ever-growing numbers. Nearly every city and town has several weight-training centers from which to choose, and the dungeon exercise rooms of the "Y" are attracting a new and larger crowd. Physical fitness has been medically proved to be life-enhancing. Strength is a major component of total fitness.

The value of weight training for all sports—from golf to running—is now an established fact and weight-training routines are an integral part of almost every formal athletic program. Equally important, strength has been shown to aid the optimum performance, both physically and mentally, of everyone from corporate executives to housewives.

Women, both athletes and noncompetitors, are turning to weight training to increase strength, firm up sagging muscles, and add tone and definition. Perrier's statistics show women are joining health clubs at a faster rate than men (a ratio of three to two) and the primary reason they give is the availability of weight-training equipment and instruction. And women are entering power-lifting events and physique contests that require muscular development—something that would have been unthinkable five years ago.

I'm well aware that there are many ways of achieving physical fitness. Jogging, tennis, racquetball, squash, and swimming all produce certain beneficial results. But none of these sports works on the whole body and the mind like weight training. In fact, I'm willing to say flatly that weight training, using the Mentzer Method, is the best way to build strength, endurance, and vitality, and to increase cardiovascular efficiency. Weight training is the only exercise capable of delivering all of these benefits in a safe and predictable manner.

INTRODUCTION

I want to pass on the Mentzer Method, not so you can become a competitive body-builder, but to help you achieve the state of well-being weight training can provide.

WEIGHT TRAINING FOR FITNESS

·||| Chapter 1 |||·

TOTAL FITNESS

What has brought sudden popularity to weight training, a physical-fitness activity that had taken a back seat to other forms of exercise for so many years? There are a number of reasons. Some are based on the recent advances in sports medicine and work physiology, some are the result of more enlightened thinking by physical educators and coaches, but the primary reason is that weight training has been singled out as *the* basic element in achieving total fitness. That's right, *the* basic element, the foundation on which a fit body is built. That will be a shocking statement for some but I'm going to prove it to you.

Let's start with fitness itself. What is it? What are the components of fitness? What is total fitness?

There is some disagreement on the definition of fitness, but few would dispute medical authorities who say fitness is "heart fitness." After all, you can't be fit if your heart isn't fit. But the fact is, you can't hurt a healthy heart with exercise and you can't cure a sick heart with exercise either. You can strengthen a sick heart and a healthy heart but that's the extent of our own self-improvement powers.

The best definition of fitness I've found comes from the President's Council on Physical Fitness and Sports. They say fitness is "the ability to carry out daily tasks with *vigor* and *alertness, without undue fatigue,* and with ample *energy* to enjoy leisure-time pursuits and to *meet unforeseen emergencies."* Another useful description comes from the American Heart Association and includes a phrase about achieving "a state of body efficiency enabling a person to exercise vigorously for a long time period without fatigue . . ."

What's interesting is that these and other definitions of fitness are strength-related—that is, they involve skeletal muscle and heart strength. It's not surprising then that the *Physical Fitness Research Digest,* a publication of the President's Council on Physical Fitness and Sports, says the chief elements of fitness are:

1. Muscular strength—determined by a single maximum contraction of the muscle
2. Muscular endurance—the ability of the muscles to perform work
3. Circulatory-respiratory (cardiovascular) endurance—the ability of the large muscle groups to perform moderate contractions for relatively long periods of time

The other component of fitness, according to the *PFRD,* are motor fitness or coordination, muscular power, agility, speed, and flexibility. Anyone who can put all these elements together is in very good shape indeed.

The thread that is woven through all these physical qualities is strength. Here's why. Muscular strength and muscular endurance are virtually the same thing. Improvement in muscular endurance is directly related to muscular strength and, of course, strength is a developmental trait that can be improved with the right kind of exercise. What is that exercise? Weight training.

Strength and endurance increase when repetitive exercise is performed against resistance. That improvement in strength and endurance is directly proportional to the amount of resistance, the frequency of training, and the length of the training session. Stress is crucial, since mere repetitions of muscular contractions that put little stress on the neuromuscular system have little effect on the development of strength in the skeletal muscles. What this means is that running or swimming long, slow distances, or lifting the same amount of weight time after time, doesn't provide sufficient stress to build strength—the major component of fitness. Only progressive weight training can overload the muscles, force them to work harder, and stimulate their growth.

Let's look back for a minute at the elements of *total* fitness— muscular strength, muscular endurance, circulatory-respiratory (cardiovascular) endurance, motor fitness or coordination, muscular power, agility, speed, and flexibility.

We've defined three of these factors, but what do the others mean?

Motor fitness is the ability to perform complex physical tasks with skill and physical coordination. Muscular power is the ability to release maximum muscular force in the shortest time. Agility is speed in changing body position or direction. Speed is the rapidity with which successive movements of the same kind can be performed. And flexibility is the range of movement in a joint or sequence of joints.

It's obvious that strength is necessary, and as the *PFRD* says, "Strength development may be considered not only a physical fitness need but fundamental to the total physical being."

Let me step back just a minute for a disclaimer. I don't mean to say that weight lifting is the only way to get fit. I ride a bike, I run, I swim, and in the past, I've played football and baseball. I think there is value in all types of active physical exercise. What I am saying is that weight training which follows the Mentzer Method develops all the components of physical fitness enumerated by the sports medics and the physiologists. That includes cardiovascular fitness, which I'll explain a little later. I don't think any other type of exercise will provide this total fitness.

Of course, there are some nonmedical elements of fitness as well. Fitness can be as much a state of mind as a state of actual health. If you feel good, you're probably fit enough. On the other hand, if you feel irritable, lethargic, a little overweight, and slightly out of shape in general, you probably are less than fit.

You can go to a doctor and, unless something is really wrong, you'll undoubtedly get a clean bill of health. But good health doesn't have to equal fitness. Blood-pressure readings, electrocardiograms, and stress tests aren't conclusive health indicators. Such tests can give false results and clinical experience has shown that more than half of the people who have suffered heart attacks have had normal resting EKGs in their most recent examinations.

·‖‖ Chapter 2 ‖‖·

WHAT WEIGHT TRAINING CAN DO FOR YOU

With all this evidence to support the case for weight training, what exactly can you expect if you undertake a serious exercise program that includes weight training as its major component?

The most obvious answer is increased skeletal muscular strength that will enable you to perform life's everyday tasks with greater ease. The other dividends we've mentioned include greater muscular endurance and power, which influences the ability to use strength over a longer period of time.

But we haven't discussed how weight training affects the other elements of total fitness.

Weight lifting isn't a skill sport like baseball. It doesn't take much more coordination to lift a barbell than it does to run. If you can walk, you can run, and unless there is some physical infirmity, you can also lift weights. There is a certain amount of skill involved in following the correct lifting style and in balancing and maintaining control over the weights while you exercise. These can be quickly learned. The motor benefits, however, come from the increased strength that can stabilize the joints, ligaments, and tendons that aid in all movement and improve posture, which, in turn, influences overall body balance and control.

Muscular power is another story. Obviously increased strength means increased power. One of the standard tests used for measuring muscular power is the standing broad jump. Experiments have shown that work with weights, even for a short time, can markedly increase the distance achieved in the standing broad jump. The same is true for vertical jumping, another test of power. Many basketball teams now use weight training and certain specialized machines to increase the vertical jumping ability of their players.

Probably the oldest myth about weight work is that increased muscular size makes you musclebound. The idea is patently ridiculous but the public perception is so firmly held, even today, that I'm continually asked if it's really the case.

Over the years, several researchers have set out to prove the point one way or the other. In the early 1950s, Dr. Peter Karpovich, a physiologist at Springfield College, tried to prove that weight lifters were, in fact, musclebound. Using the 1950 National AAU weight-lifting competitors and a group of college physical-education students, he designed a series of tests of flexibility. Karpovich defined flexibility as the degree to which a joint is free to move through its normal range of motion. The research discovered that the flexibility of the weight lifters was greater than that of the phys-ed students. Karpovich concluded that weight training that involves a full range of motion contributes positively to flexibility.

A more recent study conducted by Dr. James Peterson at the U.S. Military Academy at West Point found that highly trained athletes who began a systematic program of weight training were able to increase their flexibility in a matter of only six weeks. Peterson said, "The results provide formidable support for the contention that strength training, when properly performed, can in fact increase flexibility."

In another study the flexibility of two men, a body-building champion and a well-known weight lifter, was compared with the flexibility of college baseball, basketball, track, and swimming athletes. The weight trainers both scored higher than the basketball and track athletes and only slightly lower than the swimmers and the baseball players.

In the end, no more proof is needed than to look at professional sports teams that are currently using weight-training programs for their players. Virtually all football teams have a weight specialist on the staff, and most baseball, hockey, and basketball teams encourage weight training to improve strength and endurance.

If these people were worried about a loss of flexibility they wouldn't even consider toying with weights. Obviously they see the benefits.

Agility and speed are closely related and both can be readily improved by weight lifting. The general belief that weight training decreases speed of movement is related to the musclebound idea, which, as we have seen, is untrue. Here too, there is a reliable body of research. In one experiment, a specially constructed, electrically timed instrument was designed to measure speed in rotating a handle. Of the six hundred men who participated in the test, half had been lifting weights for at least six months. The weight-lifting group was significantly faster in completing the twenty-four rotations of the handle necessary to get a measurement of speed.

Another study compared a Mr. America, an Olympic weight-lifting champion, and a man who had trained with weights for only six weeks to the national norms in speed for sixteen-year-old boys. The results were amazing. The Mr. America equaled or exceeded the boys on twenty-four of thirty measurements, the Olympic champion on twenty of thirty, and the weight trainer on twenty-seven of thirty tests.

The overall conclusions reached by these studies indicated: "The concept that weight training causes a musclebound condition has proven to be a myth. Habitual weight trainers and athletes generally have greater flexibility and speed of movement than normal groups of sixteen-year-old boys."

If all of these benefits aren't enough for one fitness activity, there's more. Weight training, done in the Mentzer Method, can improve cardiovascular fitness, reduce body fat and increase lean muscular mass, reduce mental and emotional stress, and give you a new, improved physique.

·▌▌▌ Chapter 3 ▌▌▌·

CARDIOVASCULAR FITNESS

Even advocates of weight training over the years were convinced that weight training does not increase circulatory-respiratory fitness because the duration of the movements involved is too short to promote a training effect for the heart muscle. Since heart attack and heart disease are the most critical medical problems in this country, it's natural for people to look for an activity that can improve the heart. The heart must be able to pump blood and distribute oxygen efficiently for everyday activity as well as bursts of energy needed to meet those little emergencies that take place from time to time.

Of course, there are a number of factors that contribute to greater risk of heart attack and heart disease. These include heredity, age, smoking, overweight, inactivity, high cholesterol levels, diabetes, life-style, and being male. Heredity, age, and sex are factors that can't be changed, but it's possible to control all the other elements and, in fact, seven out of the nine risks can be self-inflicted.

Medical researchers aren't taking a firm stand on the issue yet, but the evidence does indicate that regular, prolonged, hard exercise may reduce the occurrence or severity of coronary heart disease. Here are the current medical findings.

Physical activity may increase heart efficiency, blood vessel size,

25

coronary collateral vascularization, efficiency of blood distribution and return, arterial oxygen content, blood volume, tolerance to stress, and joy of life.

Activity may decrease levels of serum triglycerides and cholesterol, obesity, arterial blood pressure, heart rate, and strain associated with psychic stress.

All of this is life-enhancing, and the only way of achieving these improvements is through vigorous exercise.

All active exercise places a strain on the heart, the body's most important muscle. A biceps the size of a grapefruit won't do you a bit of good if your heart muscle gives out. This is the prime concern of the people who have recently taken to the jogging and bike paths. During active exercise the heart will have to increase its normal action of 60 to 90 beats per minute to as many as 175 to 180 beats a minute depending on the stress of the exercise involved.

Any exercise program that doesn't recognize that the heart is the key to fitness is missing the mark. In fact, physical fitness implies the ability of the heart to pump and circulate blood throughout the body without strain. The fact that the heart is itself a muscle and can be trained is the basis for all cardiovascular exercise. And like all other muscles the heart can be trained and strengthened only when it is required to do stressful work. Running, biking, swimming, and weight training can strengthen the heart and increase its ability to do work.

The reason for this is something called the "training effect," which has popped into the language in the past few years like a new discovery. The training effect—the amount of exercise necessary to condition the entire cardiovascular system—was discovered in 1931 by physiologists in Scandinavia. Their extensive experiments showed that continued exercise with the same work load resulted in a gradually lowered heart rate. By increasing the work load it became easier for the trainees to handle the amount of the original work load with a heart rate that was still lower. The conclusion they reached was that a "training effect" or an adaptation takes place when the body is continually stressed, and equally important, that after adapting to a given amount of work, it's necessary to increase the training load for further improvement.

Later work by exercise physiologists indicated that whatever the activity, it had to be intense enough to raise the heart rate to at least 60 percent and preferably 80 percent of maximum aerobic power to gain the effect desired. This figure varies with the individual and with age, but it holds true generally. Maximum aerobic power is the amount of oxygen the exerciser is capable of taking in during exercise. It is the point where the

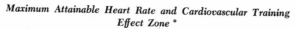

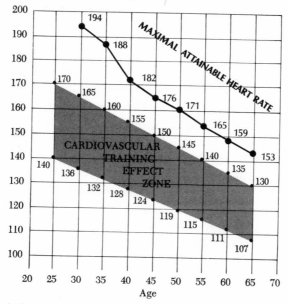

Maximum Attainable Heart Rate and Cardiovascular Training Effect Zone °

° Adapted from *Exercise Your Way to Fitness And Heart Health*, American Heart Association and President's Council on Physical Fitness and Sports, 1974.

heart can no longer pump oxygen-carrying blood to the bloodstream fast enough to create energy for further work. If you persist in maintaining the maximum level, you reach the point of exhaustion.

Since the training effect is the desired result of exercise, it's important to be able to figure your maximum rate and to know how long you must maintain the 60 to 80 percent level of activity to receive some benefit. To figure your maximum attainable rate, use the base figure of 200 beats per minute and subtract your age in years. (Some say that the figure 220 should be used as the base, but for our purposes, 200 is a better figure and it gives a much more realizable target zone.)

Thus, if you are thirty years old, your maximal heart rate will be 170 beats per minute (200 minus 30), and you'll get a training effect at 60 to 80 percent of that rate, 102 to 136 beats per minute (60 to 80 percent of 170). To be effective, this rate has to be maintained 12 to 15 minutes during each workout. For a long-range effect on heart fitness, you should strive to achieve this level or target zone of intensity three to four times a week. (See the chart.) It's the intensity level that really matters, since physical activity is not synonymous with physical training. The person who jogs once or twice a week at a slow pace, the golfer who rides in a golf cart, the tennis player who plays an occasional game of doubles are all exercising. But none of these people are exposing the heart to a load of sufficient intensity, duration, or frequency to produce a training effect.

Most people feel the same is true of weight training. It is exercise, but it can't possibly have a training effect. Traditionally, weight lifters do a set of exercises in which they raise their pulse rate rapidly to a high level, and then let it fall by taking a two-, three-, or even five-minute rest between sets of lifts. The pulse rate falls rapidly, to about half of its raised level, in as little as six seconds. Obviously, weight lifting with long rests may produce enormous skeletel muscle benefits, but the popular perception is accurate: It doesn't train the heart.

The Mentzer Method, however, is constructed so you can vary the level of intensity to a point when there is little or no time between exercises and the cardiovascular training effect can be achieved and maintained. Only progressive resistance exercise can train the skeletal muscles and the heart. The problem is, to the general public, weight training still means the development of skeletal muscles only, the kind of development exemplified by the Mr. America physique. I developed my method with the express intent of revolutionizing weight training and creating an exercise regime that would be all-inclusive as a body and heart builder. I also want to change the public's mind about weight training and show that resistance exercise affects the whole person, both physically and mentally.

But back to the question of cardiovascular fitness and weight lifting. Dr. Per-Olof Astrand, one of the world's foremost work and exercise physiologists, says, "Cardiac output is in many types of exercise similar," and that "rhythmic muscular contractions will squeeze out blood from the veins" and raise the effective pressure of blood flow. Astrand goes on to say, "Practical experience has shown that work with large muscle groups for three to five minutes followed by rest or light physical activity for an equal length of time, then a further work period, is an effective method of training the heart. The tempo does not have to be maximal during the work periods." Astrand also found that short bursts of energy, maintained for as little as one minute, seemed to produce a training effect. His major finding for our purposes, however, is that nonstop rhythmical activity for short periods of time puts the greatest demand on the cardiovascular system.

Dr. Peterson's program at West Point took measurements of cardiovascular fitness in addition to the flexibility measurements mentioned above. His intensive, six-week program used only weight training

(Nautilus machines) and his work was conducted with an already highly trained group of football players.

Peterson concluded in his report, "The results were conclusive. It was demonstrated that a strength-training program, when properly conducted, can have a positive effect on the central components of physical fitness." He went on to say, "Contrary to widespread opinion, not only will strength training produce increases in muscular strength, but also will significantly improve an individual's level of cardiovascular conditioning." And most importantly, "The data suggest that some of these cardiovascular benefits (sixty separate measurements) apparently cannot be achieved by any other type of training."

My own experience with Dr. Paul DeVore, a Washington, D.C., physician specializing in weight control and physical-fitness programs, was similar. My role in the privately financed research project was to supervise the exercise programs of patients who came for a variety of reasons, including hypertension and obesity. We used a weight-training program in an effort to help control most of the ailments presented by a cross section of patients.

I developed an exercise prescription for each patient based on age, heart condition, and general fitness level. Initial tests were made; then the exercises were performed under supervised conditions for eight weeks, three times a week. Stretching exercises were combined with barbell and dumbbell work. In every case there was a marked increase in cardiovascular fitness of the people in the program.

There are other examples but they all reach roughly the same conclusion: Weight work benefits the heart.

There is one caveat that needs to be mentioned here. Weight lifting can be dangerous for people who have high blood pressure, are greatly overweight, have a known heart condition, or have a family history of heart problems. A person with any of these problems should see a doctor before taking part in any exercise program, especially weight training.

BODY COMPOSITION

Weight training in particular, and exercise in general, can change body composition—that is, the relation of body fat to lean body mass. Men have about 15 percent body fat and women about 25 percent, some of which is necessary, but most of which can be safely eliminated, since body fat serves little useful purpose. One of the primary studies in the field found that intensive physical training "causes a depletion of excess fat" and that an "increase in lean body weight is attributed to muscular hypertrophy (muscular growth)."* Since the accumulation of body fat usually accounts for weight gain, this adjustment is a positive development. It also has been proven that exercise can have a favorable effect on body composition with or without change in body weight. On the other hand, it's possible to increase caloric expenditure sufficiently by means of regular exercise alone to produce a marked decrease in body weight.

Many of the research programs that produced weight loss and increase in lean body mass used running, calisthenics, and biking as the means of increasing physical activity. But several experiments have used progressive weight training. Four studies showed conclusively that "both men and women substantially increased their lean body weight and decreased their absolute and relative body fat" with significant reductions in skinfold and girth measurements. The researchers concluded, "High-resistance weight training can enhance body composition." They went on to say, "Progressive weight training programs resulted in desirable changes of body composition in six to ten weeks of time. These changes were reflected in skinfold reductions, in decreases in absolute and relative fat and in increased lean body weight."†

---

* *Physical Fitness Research Digest*, President's Council on Physical Fitness and Sports, Washington, D.C. Series 5, No. 2, April 1975.

† Ibid.

·||| Chapter 4 |||·

INJURY REHABILITATION AND PREVENTION

Ever since DeLorme and Watkins developed their weight-training program for the rehabilitation of war casualties in the 1940s, their concept, or variations on the theme, has been used for rehabilitation of athletic injuries and, under enlightened physicians, for the general public as well. Interestingly, the routines developed by these two physiologists are roughly the same as those used by weight trainers for the development of skeletal muscles that are not injured.

DeLorme and Watkins organized a group of three sets of ten repetitions for each muscle group. The sequence moved from lighter to heavier weights in each set, whether the starting weight was measured in ounces or in hundreds of pounds. The fact is, these exercises, performed by a healthy exerciser, actually serve to prevent injuries to muscles, tendons, ligaments, and joints. One of the concerns voiced by beginning weight trainers, and one of the misconceptions surrounding the sport, is that it's easy to injure yourself training with weights. Quite the opposite is true. Weight lifting is statistically one of the safest sports around. When compared with running, weight lifting is positively therapeutic. The facts are documented in a survey of 31,700 men participating in weight lifting on a regular basis. The results, reported by the *Journal of Physical*

31

Education, showed a total of 494 injuries or 1.5 percent in a one-year period. Nearly 200 of these injuries were back and wrist problems and none was heart-related.

By way of comparison, a survey of 800 runners, cited by orthopedist Dr. James D. Key, focused on running-related injuries that kept people from running for two weeks or more. The results were shocking: A total of 17.9 percent had knee problems; another 14 percent had Achilles tendon trouble; shin splints hit 10.6 percent; foot problems downed 6.9 percent; the ankle toll was 6.4 percent; 4.9 percent had fractures of the foot; calf muscles, heels, hips, and thighs accounted for another 10.5 percent; 1 percent even had fractures of the major bones of the leg. This is a total of 72.2 percent (578 people) in a single year. It's no wonder running has spawned its own network of sports medicine facilities whose primary concern is treatment of running injuries.

It's my own feeling that a major reason for the new popularity of weight training is the running boom itself. Reputable sources estimate there are as many as seventeen million runners and joggers who regularly pound the pavements and the tracks, endlessly circling in a search for fitness which will insure long life and happiness. Unfortunately, running, as good as it is for your heart, also has a tendency to tear the rest of the body apart. Show me a runner who hasn't sustained some kind of injury in the past year and I'll show you someone who isn't putting in very many miles.

What I'm saying is that many people, after running for four or five years, and suffering a variety of injuries from blisters to stress fractures, have decided that there are other ways to get fit and stay that way. These people have either abandoned running or started to run less and play tennis or racquetball, ride a bike, or lift weights. They probably still run, but, tired of spending a lot of time on the injured list, they have opted for something they think will keep them fit and off the injured list at the same time.

In the case of running, there are three roles for weight training. The first is increasing overall strength, the second is injury prevention, and the third is rehabilitation. The basic resistance exercises described in later chapters are widely used for rehabilitation of pulls, strains, and breaks, but weight training is highly useful in preventing injuries as well. I run, bike, and play tennis and I used to play baseball, and I have suffered only one serious injury, a result of carelessness rather than physical breakdown. At no time have my knees given away, my ankles been sprained, or my back thrown out, and I simply cannot attribute that to a naturally solid bone and muscle structure. I know that this is the result of weight training over a number of years. The reason that so many professional sports teams—in baseball, football, hockey—are using weight training today as part of their regular conditioning routines is not solely because they want their players to be stronger (although that is certainly one result), but also because they want to prevent the million-dollar running back from twisting a knee and ending a career.

·‖‖ Chapter 5 ‖‖·

RELIEF OF STRESS

To me total fitness includes the mind as well as the body, and the Mentzer Method is designed to relieve mental stress, which Dr. Hans Selye says leads to physical malfunctions. Selye maintains that everything from heart attacks to alcoholism and obesity can be caused by stress and that the relief of stress can go a long way toward eliminating such problems.

It's obvious that skeletal muscle strength, endurance, cardiovascular fitness, flexibility, and nutrition are integral to physical fitness, but mental well-being also plays a major role in the total outlook of even the fittest athlete.

This concept is not really new. Mind-body relationships have been recognized for thousands of years. The Greeks knew a healthy body combined with a healthy mind presented an ideal specimen. Wilhelm Reich felt that physical problems—hypertension, asthma, rheumatism, even ulcers—were often the results of chronic mental anxiety. And Selye's stress studies in the 1930s caused him to add migraine headaches, neck pain, obesity, and heart attacks to Reich's list of stress-related physical ailments. Per-Olof Astrand feels it is logical to assume that the reverse situation is also often true—that psychological changes result from physical changes. This is supported by the response of people to the 1979 Perrier Fitness Study, which showed that those people who exercise and participate in sports on a regular basis feel better in general, sleep better, are less tense, and are better able to cope with the pressures of daily living. Psychologist Bruce Ogilvie has reported that his tests on a cross section of athletes found them to be in an exceptionally good state of mental health.

There is no doubt that the stress of life in the twentieth century is difficult to handle for many people, and those who can afford it discuss their problems with psychiatrists, or take a cornucopia of depressants and/ or stimulants. Our stomachs seem to be continually upset, our heads ache, we can't sleep, we overeat or undereat. "Pressure" is a common complaint and people are likely to tell you without any prompting that they are under a lot of stress.

What is stress really and how do we get rid of it? Hans Selye, the pioneer and acknowledged expert in the field of stress research, defined stress as "the nonspecific response of the body to any demand." The body's reaction to this is what Selye called the "General Adaptation Syndrome" (GAS), a three-level response that begins with an alarm followed by resistance and concluded by a state of exhaustion. The stress itself causes internal chemical reactions that include the release of adrenaline, a faster heart rate, faster reflex speed, muscle tenseness, and speeded-up thought processes.

People associate stress with work and noise, but stress is also caused by intense exercise, the threat of physical danger, an injury such as a cut finger, or the sight of an old friend. Selye says the body reacts the same to pleasure and success, failure and sadness. Both "good" and "bad" can and do cause stress and, in fact, everyone is under some degree of stress even when asleep. Stress is the wear and tear a body handles, and its effects depend on how we adapt and how we dissipate its accumulation of energy.

Stress isn't a new phenomenon, either, it just has a different name. Around the turn of the century, people were faced with the same problems we seem to think are the result of modern life. They had problems on the job, they had to dodge the horse and carriage in the street, they got sick, they laughed and cried. Our stress today is no less severe and maybe it is more pervasive but the problem is we have fewer ways of dissipating its effects. Our GAS is always in operation, often on an emergency basis, but unlike our turn-of-the-century counterparts, the physical outlets for dissipating stress are not built in. Physically we are cared for, there is no need to stoke the furnace or even walk to work. The outlets for our pent-up emotions then become internal, and the evidence of tension can be seen in what Selye calls "the diseases of civilization," from asthma to heart attack and sudden death.

Clearly these dammed-up emotions have to be released on a regular basis, and exercise is the means to that end. Most active exercises can reduce the tension level in the body but weight training is unique in that it can be pinpointed to the area where the stress is located, often in the neck, the back, the stomach, and the shoulders.

This may sound like a popular television commercial but there is more pain reliever for tension headaches, and a good deal more pleasure, in twenty-five sit-ups than in two aspirin tablets. Exercises can be designed to provide immediate relief for tension in the neck, the shoulders, and the abdomen. In fact, most of the exercises described in later chapters of the book are also ideal for relieving specific areas of tension as well as that generalized feeling of the blahs that results from daily wear and tear.

OTHER ADVANTAGES

Quite aside from all the obvious physical benefits of weight training we've just discussed, there are some other tangible advantages that are more psychological than physical.

First, as I've said, weight lifting for fitness is an activity that requires very little skill. It doesn't take much practice, and in fact it's one of those rare sports that you actually can do well the very first time.

It's also a private activity, and like running, the competition is only against yourself. Weight training is convenient; you don't even have to go out in bad weather. Workouts are short, and results are quick to reveal themselves. There is virtually no way to be unsuccessful unless you're just dabbling, and then no exercise program can help you. It's also a highly motivating form of exercise because you can actually see results as well as feel them. And it's the type of exercise you can carry on throughout life.

I don't think I can overstate the case for the overall medical benefits of weight training. I know that most people have their favorite exercise activity, but consider this: From cardiovascular fitness to muscular strength, to endurance, to flexibility, to prevention of and rehabilitation from injury, to the relief of mental stress, weight training can do it all, and it's the only method of exercise that combines all the components of total fitness.

·‖‖ Chapter 6 ‖‖·

STRENGTH IS IMPORTANT

The value of weight training for all sports—from golf to running—is now an established, and weight-training routines are integral parts of most formal athletic programs in high school, college, and the professional ranks. This is a relatively new development, but the results can be documented in the continuing flow of new records in track and field, swimming, the exceptional performances of gymnasts, the phenomenon of the "little" man hitting the tape-measure home run, and middleweight weight lifters shattering the records set by heavyweights just a few years ago.

Most outstanding athletes now use a scientifically designed weight-training program for developing strength and endurance, and they use it in season and out. Considering this general popularity, what took so long for strength training to reach its current level of acceptance in the sports world?

The main reason has been the resistance of the coaching profession, in general, to the importance of strength in sports. The myth of the musclebound weight lifter has become embedded in the collective minds of the coaching profession and physical-education teachers. Both groups should have known better.

Strength is one of the major elements in good athletic performance. The other elements—speed, mobility, flexibility, endurance, and coordination—correlate with an individual's muscular strength. Strength development is considered not only a basic physical-fitness need but also fundamental to total athletic development. It's also well documented now that people with greater muscular strength have greater muscular endurance.

It's interesting, then, that up until the 1970s most coaches in all sports and at all levels resisted weight-training programs for their athletes, even athletes engaged in events like the shot put and the discus throw, where strength is such an obvious asset. Some coaches even had rules forbidding their players from working out with weights during the season and didn't take kindly to the idea even when players were free during the off-season. This prohibition was particularly true in football for some reason, a sport where whole-body strength and power are vital to good performance. Gene Hooks, director of athletics at Wake Forest University, goes all the way, saying, "Strength is the key to success in modern athletics. The coach who capitalizes on this knowledge is destined for success. The coach who doesn't is destined for mediocrity."

Some theories have been developed over the years to explain this lack of interest (and sometimes adamant resistance) to a training regime that seems so obviously important and so demonstrably successful.

Terry Todd, director of the National Strength Research Center at Auburn University and a former world power-lifting champion, has his pet theory. Todd says, "In the old days there were a number of professional strongmen and they were generally just naturally strong, ponderous, and big-boned. They looked slow-moving and thick, though they weren't, and the conclusion drawn was that weight lifting would make you a draft horse instead of a racehorse. Coaches and other people involved in athletics wanted a different result from their training. There was certainly no evidence other than exceptional size to cause people to conclude that these big men were too large to be fast, but the conclusion was drawn anyway."

The truth is, of course, that there have been some very large athletes who were very quick, agile, fast, and strong. Todd says, "It's just easy to look at a man like Louis Cyr [a 350-pounder billed as "The Strongest Man Who Ever Lived" in the 1930s] and say to yourself that the man can hardly walk, so how could he run? But, in fact, Cyr could hold a broomstick in his hands and jump through it. Many of these early strongmen were tested at the time and found not to be wanting, but rather to be superior in athletic skill."

Bob Hoffman, the founder of the York Barbell Company and the York Barbell Club weight-lifting team, wrote back in 1939: "Unfortunately in the beginning of weight lifting in this country, most of the lifters were huge, beefy men of the Continental type. They were strong, usually fat. This gave the sporting writers of the newspapers, who to a large degree mold public opinion, the belief, which they continued to foster through their writings, that weight lifting was responsible for the physical condition of these men."

Of course, there were exceptions. Eugene Sandow, the man credited with popularizing body-building in this country, was extremely muscular at 180 pounds. Single-handedly, Sandow probably did the cause of physical training more good than any other man, but his influence wasn't enough. As Hoffman said, the huge, corpulent men with tremendous appetites caused "the world's best form of exercise to be unfairly maligned, stigmatized as a sport which will ruin its devotees physically, building fat, ugly, misshapen bodies, with weak hearts and hardened arteries."

Hoffman's appraisal of the public-relations situation was probably accurate. At the very least, the outward appearance of men like Cyr, Horace Barre, Carl Moerke, and others was forbidding and caused professional coaches and trainers to look to other training methods.

Terry Todd has another theory, which revolves around the coaching profession itself. Todd says, "One prominent college coach told me recently that coaches are much more resistant to weight training than the athletes on their teams. This coach said there are still a lot of professional and college coaches who were not weight-trained when they were active players and they just aren't comfortable teaching it. This means they have to give the responsibility to someone else and this can, and sometimes does, divide a player's loyalties. The other side of that coin is that some coaches know just enough, and trust weight training enough, to be dangerous. They want to be the teachers, but they don't know which exercises are best, how they are supposed to feel when done correctly, and what the results should be. This creates other problems because then the routines they use don't really produce much in the way of results and the whole thing becomes a self-fulfilling prophecy."

It's interesting that while weight training for team and nonteam sports was languishing in this country despite the heroic efforts of such men as Bob Hoffman and others, European coaches were embracing strength training in all sports and began to produce big, powerful men and women who also were fast and agile.

And this "recent" discovery of the value of resistance exercises by American athletes, teams, and coaches is only a rediscovery of what many athletes have known for a long time.

Back in the 1940s, Emil Zatopek, the great distance runner, devised his own program of weight training and made enormous progress in a short time. Sprinters like Mal Whitfield and field athletes like Parry O'Brien trained heavily with weights. Frank Stranahan, one of the world's top amateur golfers in the 1950s, was an avid weight lifter who openly advocated his training methods. The Reverend Bob Richards, the premier American decathlon performer in the 1940s and 1950s, used strength training for all his events and used weights extensively for rehabilitation. The Australian tennis team, German swimmers, and gymnasts from all countries used weights for training long before they became acceptable to coaches in this country.

In the meantime, research has been continuing, and what has been empirically understood by many in the past has now been confirmed.

Studies in the speed of movement have found:

- Consistent weight lifters have greater speed in rotary movements of the arms and shoulders than non-weight lifters.

- Speed improves in proportion to the amount of overload involved in the resistance exercise.

- Speed of movement follows the improvement of muscular strength and muscular endurance.

In the area of muscular power:

- Strength development programs result in significant improvement in muscular power, including higher vertical jump and longer standing broad jump, shot put, and basketball shot for distance.

- Circulatory-respiratory endurance is increased by resistance exercise so that experimental groups who run and are weight-trained far exceed in performance those who only run.

In specific sports the story is the same: In baseball, speed and velocity in throwing the ball improve with weight training; in swimming, times are reduced; in football, the speed and force of the line charge improve; in football, basketball, and track, motor fitness (measured by strength, power, and endurance) improve signicantly in the short run and in the long run.

Physical Fitness Research Digest says the implications of such findings are:

1. Progressive weight-training programs are superior forms of training.

2. Strenuous resistance exercises are needed for best results.
3. Exercise programs designed to strengthen muscles primarily involved in a particular sport can be used as supplements to regular practice in effectively improving the athlete's skills and motor fitness.

All of this should warm the cockles of any coach's heart and the heart of anyone participating in team or individual sports—anyone, that is, who wants to improve. The rest of the story is that progressive resistance exercise is quick, relatively painless, and absolutely effective for virtually everyone who sticks with it for at least six weeks.

·||| Chapter 7 |||·

FACT AND FICTION

Muscular development and definition are looked on with awe, interest, envy, and even excitement, but only a few people will look at the highly defined physique and call it attractive. I happen to think that the finely tuned body of an athlete—man or woman—is infinitely more attractive than an untrained body. And I have a feeling that the main reason bodybuilders have suffered public and private criticism and scorn for so long is that people are just downright jealous of a person who has taken the time and energy to reach a level of physical fitness that few will ever know. To my mind, it is this jealousy that has helped create the mist of myth and misconception that obscures many of the benefits of weight lifting with a series of manufactured charges that are completely unfounded in fact but that have endured for decades. Some progress toward the truth has been made in the past ten years, but some of the myths remain and they are still powerful enough to keep many people away from the barbells and thus deprive them of a beneficial and rewarding experience.

No doubt you have heard or read that weight lifting is great if you want to build muscles (that point has never been denied), but that if you keep working with weights:

- It can make you musclebound and inflexible.

- It does nothing for the heart.

- It can injure you permanently.

- You get fat when you quit.

- Women will develop large muscles.

I get asked about all of these points more often than you'd believe, usually by intelligent people who have been running, playing tennis, skiing, swimming, or what have you, but have never tried weight lifting or have shied away for these very reasons. I try to answer everyone in a calm and reasoning way and here is what I tell them.

MUSCLEBOUND

This is invariably the first question people ask, and it's really laughable. The muscular body has been glorified for centuries by painters and sculptors and it's impossible to look at today's athletes in track and field strength events, in Olympic weight lifting, boxing and legitimate wrestling and gymnastics and say they are musclebound, unable to move with speed and agility because they are too muscular.

CARDIOVASCULAR FITNESS

As explained earlier, properly conducted weight-training exercises using the Mentzer Method will increase heart fitness. It is true that traditional methods of training which allow for rest periods between sets and exercises do not raise the pulse rate for a sufficient length of time to provide for a cardiovascular training effect. My method keeps you moving at a fast pace for the required twelve-to-twenty-minute period and will provide the same amount of heart training as a fast run for the same amount of time.

INJURY

I can't think of a sport that is safer than weight lifting. Runners suffer a phenomenal number of injuries, and skaters, skiers, bikers, even walkers suffer a disproportionate number of debilitating injuries. There are a number of books available that are devoted almost exclusively to the care and treatment of running injuries and, interestingly, a number of them recommend weight training as one method of rehabilitation. Well-known athletes in football, baseball, tennis, and track use weights to help strengthen weakened joints, tendons, ligaments, and muscles.

Of course, this doesn't mean you can't injure yourself lifting barbells. If you insist on living dangerously, if you don't warm up properly, if you try to impress your friends by lifting heavier weights than you're used to, you can hurt yourself. But properly performed, weight training is among the safest forms of exercise.

GETTING FAT

Before you say, "Muscle will turn to fat," let me assure you that that old saying ranks right up there with being able to change lead to gold. Even an alchemist couldn't pull it off. Old body-builders don't turn to fat when they stop working out unless they continue to eat as heartily as they did when they were training. Exercise uses calories, and heavy workouts require more energy. A training diet of 3,500 to 4,500 calories a day is not uncommon for a body-builder, but during that period he or she is probably using anywhere from 2,500 to 3,500 calories in pure energy.

That's just fine during training but, if the body-builder (or any other athlete, for that matter) retires and continues to eat as if still training, the pounds will pile up. This gives the impression of muscle having turned to fat. In reality it's just fat. The highly developed muscles of the body-builder get smaller after training is discontinued and they go back to their normal or undeveloped size.

Just as a rose is a rose, fat is fat, and muscle is muscle.

MUSCLES FOR WOMEN

Males have a hormone called testosterone that is primarily responsible for muscle development. Women don't have the same amount of testosterone and, therefore, can't develop malelike muscles.

You only have to look at the figures of some of the top women body-builders to see that the muscular development, though more prominent than on the untrained women, is still far from massive. And on close examination you can see that these women who train with weights may have developed strength but they have also developed a firm body with a tapered waist, solid buttocks, tight thighs, and flabless arms. They are actually more feminine and, in most cases, they have cut the fat content of their bodies, which further improves appearance. Remember, muscles provide curves, but fat is shapeless.

Every weight-training book I've ever seen has at least a small section that attempts to debunk these myths and separate fact from reality. But I, like all body-builders, am asked the same questions by novices and experienced weight lifters alike. I've come to the conclusion that some myths are very hard to kill whether you're using scientific research or empirical observation. I'll just keep trying.

·|||· Chapter 8 |||·

EQUIPMENT: THE CHOICES

Professional pollsters estimate that as many as ninety million people in this country have been caught up in the fitness boom and are now exercising regularly. The needs, desires, and dreams of this generally affluent group have spawned a parallel boom in fitness-related equipment, clothes, shoes, and a deluge of gimmicks, some of which look more like medieval torture devices or space ships looking for a spot to land than items that are designed to trim fat, add muscle, and allow you to kick sand in the face of the beach bully without fear of retaliation.

The sporting goods manufacturers have hired a band of clever wizards in research and development who are working feverishly in laboratories, lofts, basements, and garages to churn out an endless stream of new products that soak into an insatiable market like rain into good bottom land. There are currently hundreds of models of running shoes, scores of squeeze-crush-mash exercise devices, dozens of styles in exercise togs, and untold numbers of miscellaneous items, most of which serve no useful purpose for the exerciser.

No method of exercise has been spared, certainly not weight lifting, yet with all the innovations and space-age gadgetry, traditional barbells and the newer but thoroughly tested Nautilus and Universal equipment are still the best for increasing the size of the biceps and all the other muscles as well.

Virtually every top-strength athlete in the world built his or her body with conventional free-weight equipment—barbells, dumbbells, pulleys, benches, and inclined boards. Of course, until recently there were really no alternatives. In the past ten years, however, a marriage has been consummated between the technologists and the exercise physiologists and it has resulted in the birth of some new and highly sophisticated exercise machines. This has caused a heated controversy among the various manufacturers over the effectiveness of the different types of equipment. The argument is probably based more on economic concerns than muscular ones because the rapidly expanding market for fitness equipment is expected to top $350 million per year by 1984.

Since I'm a competitive body-builder with a vested interest in finding the most productive exercise programs, I've kept abreast of the free-weight vs. machines argument. But rather than recite the litany of facts and opinions offered by both sides, I'll describe the relative merits of the better-known exercise aids and relate their productivity to my personal experience.

Actually, my own development resulted from an eclectic use of equipment and routines, some borrowed from other body-builders, some from the muscle magazines, and some which I compiled myself. When I began training in 1963—I was only twelve at the time—I used the basic 110-pound set of barbells and dumbbells my father bought me for Christmas that year. That beginner's set has been available from the York Barbell Company for more than fifty years.

From the beginning I wanted to be the best, Mr. America and then some, so I trained regularly. Muscles didn't exactly sprout like weeds on my prepubescent body but I did make steady gains for six years using only conventional equipment.

As my muscles and strength continued to increase I had to abandon my original equipment (and the twenty-five- and fifty-pound plates I had added over the years) and move on to a big-city YMCA, where I could have the benefit of tons of weight, cable equipment, dip and chinning bars, and walls of mirrors. The "Y" also had a Universal machine that was relatively new at that time and largely unused by the regulars, who thought of the machine as a pile of hardware that took up valuable floor space. I guess I fell into that category myself, having been bred on free weights and suffering from the same ignorance of the fundamentals of productive exercise as everyone else. I ignored the machine, too, but found it intriguing.

I continued to train traditionally, but with great diligence, as if mere perseverance would be enough to increase my muscle mass. I used free weights and, as I was to learn a few years later, my methods were often counterproductive. These methods included training every day for up to four hours, the routine advocated by all the top competitors and the muscle magazines as well.

It wasn't until 1971, when I read some articles by Arthur Jones, the inventor of Nautilus equipment, that I realized there really was a science of exercise. A short time later I called Jones and after a brief telephone conversation, it became painfully apparent to me that I had grown to be a muscular man and an aspiring physique champion who prided himself on being an expert in the field, almost by accident. If I believed Jones, then I knew literally nothing scientifically valid about the hows and whys of productive resistance exercise. And as I thought about what he said, I knew he was right.

My exposure to Arthur Jones' theories started me on a headlong pursuit of the truth about exercise that included reading everything I could get my hands on that pertained in the slightest way to the physiology of exercise.

My search soon led me to DeLand, Florida, and a personal meeting with Jones. While he continued to disabuse me of my fund of misinformation about exercise and body-building, Jones showed me his Nautilus equipment, most of which was then in the prototype stage, and explained its functional advantage over barbells. He talked, I listened.

Barbells, Jones explained, were, after all, only inert chunks of iron, guided completely by the laws of gravity. And, though our body parts move in a circular or rotary fashion around an axis at the joints, barbells provide only straight-line resistance to the muscles. This means that the lifting of barbells and dumbbells provides only indirect resistance to the muscles; this resistance is greater at some points in the range of motion than at others. This provides only one element of productive exercise. The variation in resistance would be all right, Jones said, if it paralleled the natural strength curve of the muscles, but it doesn't, and this results in an incompletely developed muscle—one quite strong at some points in the range of motion and weak at other points.

Jones developed an oblong cam that gives Nautilus machines the rotary resistance that acts directly on the muscle. The shape of the cam causes the radius to change, varying the resistance as a person's available strength changes.

While no one questions the fact that the varying resistance provided by free weights is random and not in accord with the natural strength curve of the muscles, there is some disagreement in the exercise

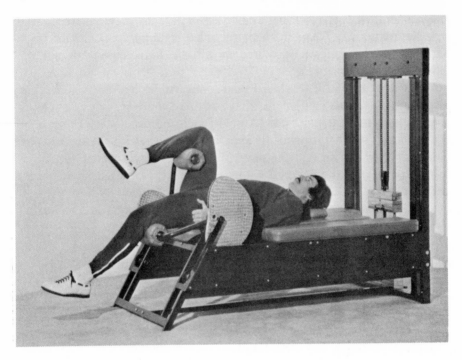

community over Jones' calculations regarding human strength curves. But even if his calculations are off somewhat, people who use his equipment will testify that the resistance it provides is more balanced than that of a barbell.

Not only must exercise provide direct resistance, but also that resistance must be applied throughout a muscle's full range of motion. This is the gospel according to Jones, but he is in substantial agreement with exercise physiologists. Nautilus equipment creates strength and muscle development evenly and uniformly as resistance is imposed from the starting point (extreme extension) of a motion through the end point (extreme contraction). Nautilus machines accomplish this by forcing the muscle to start in the fully extended position and then continue working through the full range of motion to the contracted position. This helps maintain and can even increase joint flexibility, which is an obvious advantage to any athlete.

If I appear biased in favor of Nautilus equipment it is because of the results I've obtained using it, not because I have any commercial ties to the organization. On the other hand, most of the resistance exercise equipment on the market has merit and a place in a productive exercise program. I have personally used all kinds of equipment, including some isokinetic machines and electronic muscle stimulators that are not generally available to the exercising public.

And though I believe Nautilus machines are the most scientifically based and the most productive equipment now available, they aren't magic. In fact, they require that you train extremely hard to obtain optimal results. Hard work, in fact, is the bottom line for all productive exercise. If you want to make rapid and significant increases in muscular size and strength, you have to train as intensely as you possibly can, and it makes no difference whether you're working with free weights, Nautilus or Universal equipment, or hefting Milo's legendary calf.

The type of equipment you use is at least partly determined by your training goals. It's imperative that Olympic and power lifters use free weights because the skills and techniques and the coordinated strength of the muscles required for the movements in these events can only be developed by practicing the exact lifts. These lifts eventually take place in a neuromuscular groove, and they require speed and balance. These elements are missing in the prescribed movements allowed by Nautilus and Universal equipment.

For Olympic and power lifters, the machines can be used as adjuncts, but the primary training must be with free weights.

Body-builders, however, aren't really interested in developing proper style for the prescribed lifts, or maximal strength for single-repetition lifts. For them, Nautilus and Universal machines can be used for fine-tuning individual muscles or muscle groups.

When I was in the service in the early 1970s, I was stationed at a base that had a Universal machine. That was it; there wan't a barbell in sight. And though my experience with machines was minimal, I made some of my best progress during that period. The machine was part of it, of course, but as I said before, it's hard work that produces results, and at that time I was highly motivated and trained as hard as I could.

The top physique champions, men like Robby Robinson, Boyer Coe, and Frank Zane, and the barbell manufacturers, all maintain that no recognized champion has yet used machines exclusively to develop a title-winning body. That may be true but it doesn't really prove that free weights are more productive than machines. For one thing, the machines are relatively recent innovations, while barbells have been around for decades. And second, if free weights were such powerful medicine, the rate of success among people who use them would be much higher. There are millions of body-builders all over the world but very few ever develop championship physiques.

The free-weight proponents also make another claim that is hard to substantiate. They say that people who have used machines exclusively actually lost strength when they returned to the barbells. It may, in fact, be true that a body-builder would end up being able to bench press or squat less weight than before using machines, but it isn't because the machine made him weaker. The apparent loss of demonstrable strength is due to the fact that particular lifts performed with free weights require a certain amount of skill and the coordinated use of various muscles and muscle groups. Machine exercises are performed in a controlled range of motion utilizing different muscles and neuromuscular patterns than similar exercises with barbells. What should be pointed out, but isn't, is that the same seeming loss of strength will also be detected when returning to machines after a period of work with free weights.

Until quite recently, advances in weight-training techniques were developed on a hit-or-miss basis, usually by pure accident. The vast majority of body-builders train according to tradition, convention, and imitation. Some change routines as often as they change socks. Surprisingly, some truly outstanding physiques have been developed by trial and error, and some impressive strength records have resulted from using personal routines and conventional equipment. The question is: Could the same results, or even greater results, have been achieved in less time with more sophisticated training equipment and scientifically designed routines?

The answer to that question is still unclear, but considering the recent surge in research in sports medicine, it's safe to assume that more productive training regimes and yet more space-age equipment will help the serious, and even the casual, athlete realize a greater degree of his or her potential.

There are also some practical considerations involved in the choice of exercise equipment, considerations that will dictate where and how you work out.

A full line of Nautilus machines is necessary to work the entire body. It takes twenty-three different machines to accomplish this. Universal sells machines with different numbers of exercise stations, moving up to a complete unit with sixteen stations capable of working all the muscles. Both Nautilus and Universal equipment can be productive and they are acknowledged leaders at the high end of the fitness market. These machines probably provide the fastest results possible, but obviously few people can make the investment in a complete home gym. Their prices are even prohibitive for some commercial gym facilities. Universal prices range from about $700 for the smallest unit to about $5,000 for the deluxe models. A single Nautilus machine costs about $2,000, and a full line would run as high as $30,000. If there is no price too high to pay for good health, then go to it.

But even if cost is no concern, space may be. A single Nautilus machine can fit into almost any size room, but one machine works only a few specific muscles. All the machines, as you can readily see, would take up a tremendous amount of room. A complete multistation Universal machine takes a minimum of 150 square feet and hardly fits comfortably in the average room.

This leaves conventional weights, which are much more practical for a number of reasons. First, they are very inexpensive, with a basic set of 110 pounds going for under $60. Additional weights cost from $.60 to $.80 a pound, so adding weight as needed doesn't stretch the wallet too badly. Second, free weights present no space problem whatever. You can work out in 30 square feet, and the equipment is easy to store—just stand it in the corner or push it under the bed. The cost of conventional equipment does climb, however, with your level of strength and your interest. There are benches, boards, fixed-weight dumbbells, chromed weights, pulleys, and a variety of exotic machinery that can be added. I've seen home gyms that contain only conventional equipment and that rival the most elaborate commercial gyms. This kind of setup can easily cost $10,000 and more.

FREE WEIGHTS

There is really no accurate record of the genesis of free weights that gave birth to the conventional plate-loading barbells and dumbbells in such wide use today. It is clear from drawings and writings that men and even women lifted some kind of weighted objects—stones or logs—prior to the first Olympic games in ancient Greece, and records indicate that athletes preparing for the games often lifted heavy objects as part of their training.

Weights specifically designed for lifting came into fairly common use by the muscle men and carnival performers in the early 1800s. Pulley machines were in use in the 1850s, and steel spring and rubber exercisers were developed at about the same time in France. Some of the early solid dumbbells were ingenious devices. The large iron balls on either end

could be loaded to a desired weight by adding tiny balls of shot through an opening that was sealed with a screw cap.

Progress was slow until 1924, when Bob Hoffman left the oil burner business and established the York Barbell Company in York, Pennsylvania. York barbells and the York Barbell Club quickly became synonymous with weight lifting. The York Barbell Company dominated the field until the 1970s, when the increased demand for equipment of all kinds brought new competition into the manufacture of all kinds of equipment associated with weight lifting.

The only new development of significance in the manufacture of barbells and dumbbells for home use is the vinyl-coated weight filled with a cementlike material. It is quieter and considerably cheaper than the traditional iron plates. Other than the bulky vinyl model, there have been no quantum leaps in the development of free weights. Machines obviously are a step forward for the fitness industry, but most of the really well-designed machines are too expensive for the average person and they require too much space to be useful to a mass audience.

Manufacturers of home weight-training equipment don't foresee any major design changes in free weights, and it may be true that at least in this case, "You can't gild the lily."

NAUTILUS

The first Nautilus machine was conceived in the fertile brain of Arthur Jones in the early 1940s, and a prototype machine actually was built in 1948. It took twenty-two years of research and design development to reach the point where Jones was willing to take a chance and market his invention. Interestingly, both Nautilus and Universal equipment designs seem to owe a debt to the rather ungainly equipment designed in the late 1930s by DeLorme and Watkins, who used it for the rehabilitation of World War II veterans.

Today, the company called Nautilus Sports/Medical Industries of DeLand, Florida, is a multi-million-dollar corporation that includes twenty-four hundred Nautilus Health Clubs, equipment sales, and a television operation that produces and markets fitness and medical programs.

Nautilus equipment design is based on extensive research into the precise function of each of the body's muscles and emphasizes the range of movement of the muscle from full extension to full contraction. The machines isolate and exercise specific muscle groups, even individual muscles, and control form.

To give you an example of the complexity of exercising with Nautilus, witness the instructions for use of the "Super Pullover Machine" (for the latissimus dorsi muscles of the back and other torso muscles), and note the similarity to the voice of "Mission Control" preparing astronauts for a blast-off to the moon:

1. Adjust seat so shoulder joints are in line with axes of cams.
2. Assume erect position and fasten seat belt tightly.
3. Leg press foot pedal until elbow pads are about chin level.
4. Place elbows on pads.
5. Hands should be open and resting on curved portion of bar.
6. Remove legs from pedal and slowly rotate elbows as far back as possible.
7. Stretch.
8. Rotate elbows down until bar touches stomach.
9. Pause.
10. Slowly return to stretched position and repeat.

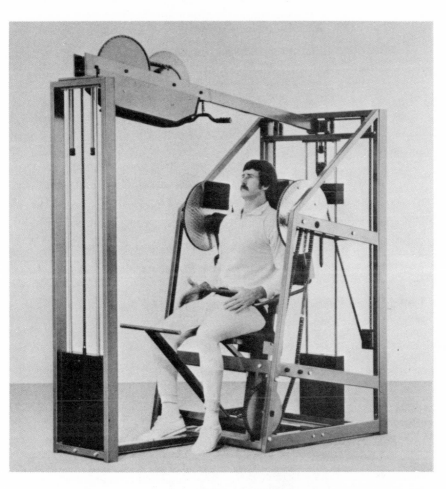

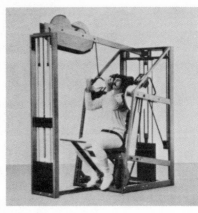

11. After final repetition, immediately do pulldown.

Important: Look straight ahead during movement. Do not move head or torso. Do not grip tightly with hands.

BLAST OFF!!

In all fairness, it's not as complicated as it sounds, but it does take some initial instruction by someone who is knowledgeable about the equipment and its functions.

Besides developing strength and thus serving to prevent sports injuries, Nautilus equipment is used in the rehabilitation of injuries.

The proof of Nautilus' success can probably be read in the phenomenal growth of the company in just ten years. Total sales of all its products passed the $300 million mark in 1981.

UNIVERSAL EQUIPMENT

Universal equipment has been on the market for more than twenty years, but until the fitness boom struck it was found mostly in school, college, and professional sports training rooms, and at many of the

progressive health spas and gyms. The firm says they used "computer-biomechanical research" to identify the human and mechanical forces involved in movement and performance.

This research, according to the company, resulted in the development of a "dynamic variable resistance" feature on their machines that automatically changes the leverage of the power exercises—presses and pulldowns—to maintain the same relative degree of muscular exertion throughout the entire range of movement. There is also independent research to show that this DVR system can produce larger strength gains than conventional barbells. Of course, as always, strength gains depend on how hard people work, and are more a function of that intensity than of any machinery.

The company offers a variety of units, from a six-station home outfit to a sixteen-station model more suitable for the gym. If space is at a premium, the basic wall-mounted model at around $700 will provide a good workout. If you have around $5,000 and at least 150 square feet of floor space, one of the multistation models with chrome plates might fill your needs. The six-station model comes with up to 260 pounds on the power stations and 115 pounds on the low and high pulley stations. The wall unit has a basic stack of 100 pounds of plates but will take the addition of two 80-pound stacks as you progress.

·|||· Chapter 9 ·|||·

TAKE INVENTORY

Realism is a major problem in the initial stages of any exercise program. Beginning runners, hikers, bikers, swimmers, and weight lifters almost invariably set goals for themselves that are simply unreachable in the short run and often unattainable in the long run as well. Not many of us are capable of a two-hour, thirty-minute marathon, climbing the Matterhorn, biking cross country, swimming the English Channel, or becoming Mr. Universe.

It's by far the better course to begin the weight-training program that follows and any other exercise program you consider, by taking inventory of your current condition, skills, genetic attributes, motivation, and available time.

Assessing your current physical condition is critical. If you have never worked with weights, you will face entirely different problems than if you have worked out before. If you have been totally sedentary for some time, you will have to take that into consideration. Overweight, high blood pressure, and body type all will influence goal setting. Your natural level of strength will dictate how much weight you can use for the suggested exercises. For women it is especially important to begin carefully, since most women simply don't have much upper body strength. Regardless of your condition, however, it's vital to remember to start slowly and give your body time to adjust to the new stress it's undergoing.

As I said before, weight training isn't a skill sport, but people with athletic ability will have an easier time in the beginning than people with little natural coordination. Don't let this part scare you, however. It's highly unlikely that you will have any trouble with the movements required regardless of your skill level. After just a couple of workout sessions you'll be performing all the exercises like an old-timer.

I'm quite aware that very few people can develop large muscular mass and that even fewer have the inclination to be a professional or competitive body-builder. But for those of you who do want to go on and develop mass and definition, it's important to know that genetics will ultimately limit such growth. Muscle fiber is what makes muscles grow. Everyone has a different fiber count, and some people have much more than others. The amount of muscle fiber is determined before birth and it cannot be changed no matter how much protein and effort you pour into it. I have seen body-builders spend endless hours in the gym, eat strange food, and pop pills in their quest for a bigger, more muscular body. I've seen some give up family, career, and education in pursuit of a title-winning physique.

In most cases this is a real tragedy, because most of them don't have the genetic makeup to become Mr. Anything. The people who develop the really massive physiques are genetically predisposed to develop large muscles. In fact, there have been a number of studies that prove an athlete's strength, speed, and endurance are matters of genetic endowment, and no amount of training can overcome a deficiency in the genes.

Per-Olof Astrand, the Swedish exercise physiologist, says "A person's potential for development of muscle strength is determined at birth . . . and remains unaltered throughout life. It may not be quite fair, but it is nevertheless a fact that the 'choice of parents' is important for athletic achievement."

Regardless of these hereditary limitations, however, it's possible for most people to make significant progress. And since there isn't a thing we can do about the limitations, there is no point in worrying about them.

Motivation is a key element in any exercise or diet program. Motivation is what causes people to take action, and it may be the most important factor in achieving success. The exercise and diet programs in this book will produce results only if you stick with them.

I think I'm highly motivated and yet there are plenty of times when I'd rather do almost anything else than work out. It's hard even for a professional athlete to keep his eye on the target all the time. The essentials of improvement are mental as well as physical.

People just love to dream when it comes to physical fitness and weight control. And it is this type of "five minutes a day to health and beauty" thinking that is the downfall of most people who want to get fit and lose some fat. It just doesn't happen overnight or without some willpower.

It's important to recognize that losing body fat and gaining muscle is a slow process. It takes weeks and even months to accumulate that extra fat and it takes the same amount of time to lose it. It takes time to lose muscle tone and development and it takes time to get it back. Be patient. Be realistic. Give yourself time to change.

It's important to be realistic on the subject of workout time as well. I'm a professional athlete, so all of my time is devoted to training. Training is my job. I get up in the morning, go to the gym for a workout, then I run, swim, and bike.

This takes care of the better part of the day, and in the time that's left I'll plan training schedules for upcoming contests, assess my diet, and just visualize my goals. Most people can't devote even a fraction of the amount of time I do to fitness, since their exercise has to be worked into a schedule that is limited by job responsibilities.

Weight training, as exercise routines go, is not very time-consuming. I recommend a twenty-minute workout, three days a week. Running, for example, can take up to two hours a day, five or six days a week. Training for a marathon can take even more time. The point is, you have to consider your available free time when planning an exercise program. If you have only a few minutes a day, so be it. But use those few minutes for all they are worth.

Weight training offers the easiest means of assessing the physical rewards of exercise—the tape measure, the mirror, and the scale. In taking inventory, it's necessary to use all of these measuring tools. It's also a good idea to keep a chart of your progress, since there's nothing quite as rewarding as looking back and seeing the figures change.

Be sure to weigh yourself on the first day and every day, but don't jump on the scale three or four times a day. Weight fluctuates almost hourly and it simply makes no sense to worry about a few ounces here and there.

Use the mirror and make an objective assessment of the way you look. Note the lumps in the wrong places and the lack of them in the right places. Rate yourself from the front and the sides and give yourself a score on a scale of 1 to 10. Be honest with yourself because you don't have to share this information with anyone else.

Finally, get out the tape measure and record your measurements.

Measure your neck, both biceps, your chest (relaxed and expanded), your waist at the navel, your hips, both thighs, your calves, and your forearms, wrists, and ankles if you want to include them. It will be great fun and a real motivator to see the changes.

·‖‖ Chapter 10 ‖‖·

THE MENTZER METHOD

One of the major problems confronting the person considering an exercise program is not so much where to find information, but how to select the program that is right for you out of all the legitimate programs available. People have been sucked in so many times, started so many regimens, and finished so few that they are naturally a little leery about taking another stab at it unless it's different and sounds logical.

Weight training, after all, isn't like running. Running style isn't a concern for most people, since everyone has his or her own. If the training routines outlined in many of the running books simply don't fit your needs, you can just go out and run. Sometimes it works and sometimes it doesn't. But the Mentzer Method, using varying intensity, will work for everyone who gives it a fair trial. It doesn't matter if you're short or tall, underweight or overweight, male or female, young or old, weak or strong. It works because it's physiologically sound. If you follow it, it will keep you in shape for a lifetime.

I want to make a point here that all too often gets covered up in the general high-pitched approach to exercise. To be effective, exercise has to be stressful. A casual bike ride may be fun, but it falls short of being a successful exercise. Weight training is probably the most stressful of all exercise programs but it is rewarding and it's fun. The fitness craze, like patent medicines, often seems to offer the dream of a fabulous return without much investment. Like anything in life, you get back what you put into weight training.

Here's a list of the things that the weight-training program I call the Mentzer Method will do for you:

- Build skeletal-muscle strength

- Increase cardiovascular efficiency

- Increase flexibility

- Take off weight

- Improve overall physical appearance

- Improve self-image

- Help prevent stress-related problems

Physical fitness has three basic components, as I explained earlier: (1) muscular strength; (2) muscular endurance or the ability to perform work on a continuous basis; and (3) circulatory-respiratory endurance or cardiovascular fitness. A good training program will meet these needs.

The Mentzer Method improves muscular strength through dynamic exercise, improves muscular endurance because athletic abilities are related to muscular strength, and improves circulatory-respiratory endurance by stimulating a cardiovascular training effect.

My method works on these three facets of fitness this way. The bouts of submaximal effort required to lift and move weights last only a few seconds, but these are long enough to develop muscular strength, tighten tendons and ligaments, and improve flexibility. When these bouts of effort last from three to five minutes, aerobic power is developed, and when maintained for twelve to twenty minutes they increase endurance by further developing the oxygen transporting system. Running and swimming, the two other inclusive methods of exercise, fall short of weight training the Mentzer way as a means to achieving total fitness because they don't build muscular strength. The Mentzer Method is therefore unique.

And there is an added dimension in weight training: the release of muscular tension through heavy physical exertion.

The Mentzer Method, however, allows you to vary the resistance of your workout to achieve any desired fitness goal—increased strength, which requires maximal or near maximal resistance for six to eight repetitions; increased cardiovascular fitness and endurance that uses moderate resistance for twelve to twenty repetitions; or total fitness, which combines moderate resistance (eight to twelve repetitions) with very short periods of rest between exercises.

DOCTOR'S EXAMINATION

As I've said, weight training is heavy exercise, and it will probably work your body harder than anything you've done recently, including running, swimming, tennis, cross-country skiing, or whatever exercise you favor on a regular basis. For this reason, and because it makes plain good sense, I strongly advise a thorough medical examination before beginning the program. You may think you're fit enough to handle this kind of routine, and maybe you are, but the prudent path leads to your doctor's door. If you're past thirty, this examination should include a stress test.

If there is any reason at all to doubt your physical condition—slightly high blood pressure, diabetes, overweight, a heart condition of any kind—or if you have a family history of any of these problems, it is very important to know that weight training demands a great deal of armwork with loads you are not used to handling. Blood pressure during armwork is considerably higher than during legwork. This forces a higher heart rate. This type of exercise is very effective in getting the blood to the heart and it creates an almost immediate increase in the heart's pumping action. For anyone with a heart problem, for older people, for sedentary people, armwork can be dangerous. Check with your doctor.

Even if you see a doctor and get approval to begin lifting weights, be conscious of any abnormal physical symptoms you experience before, during, or after your workouts. Dizziness, chest pains, and an irregular or fast heartbeat can be signs of more serious problems. If you have any doubts, stop exercising immediately. If the problems persist, then, of course, see your doctor again.

Exercise may be good for your health, but it's common sense to be careful before you start this or any other program.

Here are a few other definitions that will help you understand the Mentzer Method and get off to a flying start. You may have read and talked with your friends about some of these points before, but it's been my experience that people often think they're talking about the same thing when they really aren't.

THE OVERLOAD PRINCIPLE AND PROGRESSIVE RESISTANCE

Muscles, including the heart muscle, get stronger when they are stimulated by exercise. The reason you don't get larger muscles from your daily work load, even if it requires heavy labor, is that the load you're handling is generally the same all day long. Muscles don't develop unless you increase the load on them and then continue to increase it as you get stronger. This type of training is called "progressive resistance" training. As the resistance is progressively increased, the muscles are forced to contract maximally, and this causes them to adapt physiologically. This adaptation can be seen in hypertrophy or muscular growth.

Your fitness level is obviously important here. The more fit you are, the more intense the exercise must be to improve the level of fitness. At this stage it's very hard for me to increase my muscle mass without very intense training, and even then the gains, though significant, are relatively slight. For the average person, however, progressive resistance does produce increases in strength and development, and continued increases can come only from increasing the resistance even more. After you've been following this program for a relatively short time—a month or two—you'll develop sufficient strength to make it almost easy to do the exercises that had been difficult at first. If you could handle a given weight for six to eight repetitions at the beginning of the program, the number of repetitions you can perform will quickly increase. As a rough rule of thumb, when you can handle that same weight for ten to twelve repetitions, it's time to add more resistance. The amount of resistance (around 15 percent more) should again reduce the number of repetitions you can perform to six or eight. This same pattern should be followed in each of the exercises each time you reach a level of strength where the resistance is no longer an overload.

REPETITIONS AND SETS

There has been a good deal of research conducted to determine the optimum number of repetitions (the same movement repeated) and sets (a given number of repetitions) of exercises. The principles developed forty years ago by DeLorme and Watkins, mentioned earlier, are still generally followed in most exercise programs. DeLorme and Watkins are credited with developing the concept of "repetition maximum" (RM), which is the maximum load that can be handled in a given exercise movement before the muscles involved become fatigued. So if you can lift a hundred pounds one time, that is a 1 RM load for you. If you can lift it ten times before failure, it's a 10 RM load.

Researchers have examined the range of possible routines from one set of 1 RM loads to three sets of 10 or more RM loads. No hard-and-fast conclusions have been reached, but the optimum range seems to be three sets of 6 to 10 RM loads. It is not necessary to train at the maximum level each time you work out, however. But one session out of every three should be at maximum level to force maximum muscle exertion and growth.

Within these general guidelines lies the routine that is best for you. The only way to find out which is best is to experiment over a period of several workouts. Don't overwork yourself at first. Start with lighter weights than you think you can handle, then quickly move up to the level that provides overload. There simply is no formula for determining these things in advance.

FREQUENCY—DURATION—INTENSITY

The Mentzer Method is the only weight-training program that challenges the traditional agony of two-hour workouts, six days a week. Of course, there are variations on that theme (the "Ten Seconds a Day to Total Strength" is my favorite laugh), but no program I know advocates "intensity" the way mine does. Intensity of work load has been a hotly debated subject among professionals in the fitness world until recently. It now seems that a conclusion has been reached—namely, the greater the intensity of the exercise the better the results.

The intensity factor isn't difficult to prove to yourself. Just run uphill or run cross-country instead of on the track and you'll quickly understand that intensity is the factor that determines the way you feel at the end of your run, without regard to distance.

My definition of intensity has nothing to do with concentration and everything to do with total physical effort. Intensity of effort is two-pronged. It means taking every individual exercise to the point of muscular fatigue, that point where you can't possibly move the dumbbell or bar another inch. It also means moving from exercise to exercise with as little rest between each one as possible. This is very different from traditional weight-training routines that encourage rest periods of some length between sets, and it's also why such workouts can take as long as two or more hours. It is the continuous movement—from set to set and exercise to exercise—that keeps the intensity level high and results in the cardiovascular training effect that other regimens fail to produce.

That's my approach to intensity, but I've been training continuously for fifteen years. The beauty of the Mentzer Method is that it's infinitely adjustable. The beginning weight trainer can adjust the intensity level to meet his or her existing fitness level. This will allow the individual to achieve personal fitness goals up to maximum intensity, which provides total fitness.

Obviously, intensity has a great deal to do with duration. You can run on the flat a lot longer than you can run uphill. Your strength and energy reserves naturally limit the length of your workout. And that's the idea. Equally good results can be obtained in short, heavy workouts—heavy exercise demands a high energy supply, and that supply is limited.

Frequency of workouts is also largely determined by the intensity you bring to bear. The strength of the muscles and glycogen supplies need to be restored, and that takes time. Three twenty-minute workouts a week are all you should try and probably are all you can handle.

PULSE MONITORING

The basic requirement for increasing cardiovascular fitness is exercise that will elevate the pulse rate to your age-adjusted training level (60 to 80 percent of maximum) and keep it there for twelve to twenty minutes.

Monitoring the pulse is difficult when exercising but in weight training it's easier than in most other forms of exercise. Since you stop briefly between exercises anyway, it is possible to take a quick reading without interrupting your routine.

The artery on the thumb side of the wrist is most often used for pulse taking, but during exercise it's easier to use the large arteries on either side of the neck. To find the artery, put your thumb on your lower jaw and cup the chin in the hollow between the thumb and forefinger. The artery is just in front of the thick muscle that runs vertically in the neck. Find the pulse with your middle finger. To get an accurate count you must take a reading immediately after stopping your exercise because the rate drops very quickly. After locating the pulse, count the beat for ten seconds and multiply that number by six to get the per-minute rate.

In an untrained person the resting pulse rate should be in the 60-to-80 range, but in trained people it may be as low as 40 beats per minute. The upper, or training range, of course, is age-adjusted and can be found easily on the chart in Chapter 3.

When you start exercising you should monitor your pulse quite often to make sure you are reaching your training goal, but after a while you'll begin to recognize your body's response when your pulse rate moves into the training zone. Until that time, however, it's best to take a reading before warming up, immediately after a sequence of exercises, and then after you've cooled down. If, during the strenuous part of your routine, your pulse rate is still below 60 percent of maximum, you'll have to increase the intensity of your work. On the other hand, if you're in the 85 percent range, it is best to cut back a little on intensity.

MUSCULAR CONTRACTIONS

There are two types of muscular contractions that are important in dynamic (movement) exercise—concentric and eccentric.

In concentric movement the muscle shortens (as when you flex your biceps). The smaller the angle around the joint involved in the movement, the greater the muscular tension. Try it yourself. Pick up a light dumbbell and hold it with your arm straight down (180-degree angle). There is very light tension at that point. Now slowly raise it until your arm has curled up to 90 degrees. The tension is maximum at about that point. Continue to curl the dumbbell until your arm is flexed completely.

During the course of these exercises you'll find this to be something of a problem, because the heaviest weight you can handle is no greater than the weight you can lift at the weakest point in the range of muscular motion. You may be able to hold a fifty-pound dumbbell at any point in the range of motion, but raising it in the curl exercise will be impossible at first.

Eccentric movement or contraction is the opposite of concentric, in that the muscle lengthens rather than shortens. When you lower the dumbbell from the curled position that is an eccentric movement.

FORM

Almost every time I go to the gym I'm shocked to see even experienced body-builders performing their exercise routines in a style that is not only sloppy but also unproductive. Minor variations are certainly no problem, but when you jerk, heave, and twist when you should be straight, and apply force with the wrong set of muscles, you are actually working against yourself. The old adage, "Anything worth doing is worth doing well," applies to weight training, weight lifting, and body-building just as it does to swimming and diving.

Scientific studies have shown that barbell exercises that begin with a sudden jerk, rather than a smooth movement, and are completed rapidly, apply resistance only at the beginning and the end of the movement. Slow, smooth movements, however, apply resistance to the entire length of the muscle. Momentum is a factor, of course. It's much easier to keep a weight moving than it is to get it moving in the first place. Momentum is then substituted for muscle contraction, and the benefits are lost.

You can prove this to yourself by doing sit-ups in two ways. First, do half a dozen as fast as you can, bouncing up each time you hit the floor. Then do another six, but this time pause for a count of two when your back touches the floor. The intensity of the second movement is quite evident and you can feel it more in your abdominal muscles.

It's important then that the exercises in the routines that follow be performed from beginning to end in a controlled and deliberate fashion. The weight should leave the starting position smoothly, by pulling or pushing rather than jerking and throwing. This will force you to use muscle contraction and extension alone to move the bar or dumbbell. If you follow this form you should be able to hold the weight in its final position or stop it at any point in the range of motion of the exercise. Physiologists have proven that your ability to hold a weight is greater than your ability to lift the same amount of weight.

Controlled and deliberate performance is also an important factor in lowering the weight. Some exercise physiologists feel the negative motion (lowering the weight) is more productive than the positive (lifting the weight). This means that the weight should be under complete control at all times, even during those last two or three repetitions, which are so much more difficult.

Controlled exercise performance also serves to prevent injury. It's almost impossible to injure muscles or tendons if the weight is raised and lowered by muscular contraction only. Yanking or jerking the weight, on the other hand, can cause muscle pulls or tears and can strain tendons and joints as well.

HOW TO DETERMINE THE WEIGHT TO USE

There have been a number of attempts to create charts that would determine the amount of weight to use for each exercise, but these attempts have all ended in confusion and ultimate failure because the number of variables is too great. Body type, age, sex, strength, height, weight, motivation, and athletic ability all enter into the equation, and this makes it impossible to set norms that apply evenly to a broad range of people.

This leaves the selection of the proper weight for each exercise up to the individual, and this means experimentation. If this is your first weight-training program, you probably have no real idea of your strength—that is, you may be stronger or weaker than you think you are. Just because you can carry the groceries home from the store doesn't mean you can press forty pounds. Some of your muscles are naturally stronger than others and this makes it necessary to change weights for the different exercises in the training sessions to maintain the proper resistance for each movement.

Remember, to build strength you must use fewer repetitions and heavier weights, and to build endurance you use lighter weights with a higher number of repetitions. Thus, in selecting the weights that allow for proper performance, determine in advance if you are striving primarily for strength or endurance. (The two are not mutually exclusive, however, as both methods of training exercise the entire muscular system.) If you're in the strength category, the weight you settle on should allow for only six to eight repetitions, and if you're looking for endurance, then twelve to twenty repetitions are necessary to raise the pulse and increase cardiovascular fitness.

It's easy to kid yourself by selecting weights that are too light. If the tenth or twelfth repetition is easy, you need more weight. Then, as I've said, increase the weight as you get stronger, and the repetitions become easier.

DRESS

One of the real beauties of weight training is that you don't have to dress for it. It's an indoor activity all year round (unless you live near "Muscle Beach"), so that generally all you need is a pair of shorts, a T-shirt, and a pair of sneakers with flat soles. Comfort is the byword. Don't wear anything that constricts your movement, including support belts (stylish, but of more psychological than real use). You may want to warm up a bit in a sweat shirt and sweat pants in the cold weather, but as soon as you start working out you'll want to shed any excess clothing. The main thing is not to overdress.

BREATHING

During exercise, the body is subjected to generalized stress that is first felt in an increased demand for oxygen by all the body's tissues, but especially the muscles. To meet this need, it's necessary to breathe harder and faster.

During the first two minutes of exercise, anaerobic (the absence of oxygen) power is utilized. At about two minutes the ratio is fifty-fifty, anaerobic to aerobic (the presence of oxygen), and then shortly, the aerobic process dominates. So in the short span of two or three minutes the body is making full use of the oxygen it's taking in.

It's the aerobic zone that stimulates the cardiorespiratory training effect, and the Mentzer Method is the only weight-training program that allows you to control intensity and remain in the aerobic zone for twelve minutes or longer.

When lifting weights you should try to establish a controlled rhythm—inhale when lifting, exhale when lowering. It's a very natural process.

FATIGUE

Fatigue is caused by a drop in the level of blood sugar and the accumulation of lactic acid in the muscles. This can be a major problem in a running program but it shouldn't be of concern in a weight-training workout. You will undoubtedly be fatigued after your twenty minutes with the iron, but it should be a pleasant kind of fatigue which leaves you tired but pumped up and energetic at the same time.

The workouts are short enough to prevent any dramatic oxygen debt or lactic acid buildup and if necessary you can always stop for a minute and replenish your blood sugar with a drink of juice.

IN SICKNESS OR IN HEALTH

When the body is sick or run down the energy level is quite low, motivation to exercise is absent, and strength is reduced. If you find yourself feeling "under the weather" on a workout day, pass up the workout. If you go ahead, you will only be stretching your body's already depleted resources and you not only will have an unrewarding workout, but also you may set back your recovery time considerably.

SORENESS

If you've been sedentary for a while, any exercise, even a brisk walk, will leave you with some muscle soreness. More strenuous exercise can cause severe soreness. It's incredible that medical science can unravel many of the body's complex internal mysteries but is unable to discover the exact cause of soreness. Yet almost everyone can clearly describe the stiff, hardened feelings of sore muscles.

Sometimes when you're extending yourself, you can almost feel the soreness coming on; at other times the first symptoms don't appear until about twelve hours later. The pain gradually gets a little more severe for about twelve hours and then it begins to fade away. In a couple of days it's forgotten. Everyone experiences some soreness and it's absolutely nothing to worry about, but if it persists, just cancel your workouts until it dissipates.

·‖‖ Chapter 11 ‖‖·

GETTING STARTED

Since weight lifting is an individualized activity, you can begin at any level of strength and still reap the benefits. If you have been sedentary for a long period of time, you will have to break in more slowly than if you've kept in shape. But regardless of your physical condition, I think it's wise to begin weight training slowly and prudently, and that means five to ten workouts using very light weights or, if necessary, just the bar and the dumbbell handles. This approach serves two purposes: It helps you get used to the movements, and it keeps soreness to a minimum.

A certain amount of soreness, usually minor, is inevitable whenever you take up a new activity, because each new physical movement involves different sets of muscles moving in different patterns. In weight training you can easily control soreness because you can generally feel it coming on and can stop the particular movement. The break-in period will require keeping your enthusiasm under control and realizing that there is plenty of time for progress.

I know that restraint can be difficult, but I also know that soreness can be incapacitating, frustrating, and ultimately discouraging, and this combination can be the death knell of any exercise program.

During the break-in I think it's a good idea to work out fifteen to twenty minutes every day for at least five days. If you need more than five workouts to get ready, then take one or two days off (no more) and add another five days, but increase your training time to twenty-five to thirty minutes per session.

One set of exercises for each body part is all that's necessary during the break-in period. Each exercise should be performed twelve times (twelve repetitions), and you shouldn't be huffing and puffing to make that twelfth rep. Take your time; rest between exercises or even between repetitions, if necessary. You should concentrate on form and on maintenance of slow and steady movement. Think about what you're doing, try to feel which muscles are involved in the movements, and adjust your body as necessary because you have to feel comfortable and well balanced.

THE WARM-UP

It's essential to perform some kind of warm-up exercises before beginning any exercise routine. I prefer movements that stretch the muscles. Some people like more traditional calisthenics, yoga, or even meditation about what they are going to do.

But the fact is, active warm-up helps prevent injuries, gets the blood flowing, raises the heartbeat, raises the body and muscle temperature, and gets you psychologically ready for exercise.

The amount of warm-up necessary depends on the individual, but five minutes is probably adequate for most people. Some people take ten to fifteen minutes, and some make warming up a career. Actually, experiments have shown that more than fifteen minutes is unproductive, and if you wait more than fifteen minutes between warming up and working out, you might as well start all over again because the benefits of the warm-up have been lost. So move directly from the warm-up to the exercises.

THE COOLDOWN

After the intense exercise period, it's a good idea to spend five minutes or so doing stretching and bending exercises similar to those used in the warm-up so the body has a chance to readjust to its normal activity level. During exercise the pulse rate and oxygen intake have risen dramatically. If you stop exercising suddenly, the heart is still hard at work and continues to provide blood circulation for the working muscles. This can cause dizziness or muscle cramps. Slow down and then cool down and you won't have any problems.

WARM-UPS—FIVE MINUTES

Twist. Stand up very straight, feet about shoulder width apart. Clasp your hands behind your head and hold your elbows out to the side as far

back as you can. Twist your upper body to the left, bringing your right elbow to the front. Return to the starting position and repeat to the other side. This exercise can also be done sitting down. Repeat 15 times.

Stretch. Clasp your hands over your head with your arms stretched and elbows straight. Your feet should be about shoulder width, your back straight, and your eyes straight ahead. Bend to the right as far as possible and then to the left. Repeat 15 times to each side.

Bend. Stand straight with your feet together and your arms extended parallel over your head and your elbows close to your ears. Slowly bend at the waist and touch your toes with your fingertips. Try to keep your head between your arms all the way down. Hold for the count of 1 and return to the starting position, stretching high. Repeat 20 times.

Thrust. Stand with your hands on your hips, your back straight and your eyes front. Squat down and place your hands flat on the floor. Lean forward slightly and thrust your right leg full length in back of you. Bring it forward and repeat with your left leg. Do 15 thrusts with each leg.

Raise. Start in the squat position with your fingertips on the floor,
heels up and head up. Stand up and
straighten the knees as far as possible without taking your fingers off
the floor. Squat and repeat 20 times.

This series of five warm-ups
involves all the major muscles of the
body in a five-minute routine that is
guaranteed to get the pulse moving,
warm the muscles, and limber up
your body and mind. The same sequence can be repeated as a cool-
down routine, or you can substitute
any other routine as long as it takes
at least five minutes.

You're now ready to move on to
the break-in exercises.

·||| Chapter 12 |||·

BREAK-INS: THE BASIC EIGHT

NOTE: Use a weight for each of these exercises that allows for eight to ten relatively easy repetitions. If your muscles start to fatigue after five or six repetitions, the weight is too heavy. On the other hand, if you can do twenty or thirty reps, then the weight is obviously way too light. Make the adjustments and go to it, moving steadily from one exercise to the next.

THE BASIC EIGHT—20 MINUTES
No. 1: Full Squats

Muscles: Upper legs, lower back, upper back.
Comment: Of all the exercises in this book, this is my favorite. Squats aren't easy by any means, but that's what makes them so productive. In a short time, the thighs will show real growth and you'll feel increased flexibility in the knees. But squats benefit the back of the legs and the entire back as well, and they are good stimulators for the body because they involve most of the large muscles in one movement.
Directions: Stand with the feet comfortably spread. Make sure you have a strong, stable foundation. Bend over, flexing the knees, and grip the bar with an overhand grip, hands a little wider than shoulder width apart. Keep the head up and the back as flat as possible. Using the upper legs

and lower back, bring the bar straight up in a plane parallel with the body. Keep the arms straight until the bar passes the knees, then begin to bend the elbows and prepare to tuck them under the bar as it reaches chest level. Get underneath the bar and bring it to rest on the upper chest, just under the chin. Next, press the bar upward and then lower it behind your head so that it rests comfortably across the shoulders and the base of the neck.

Adjust the weight and your stance until you're steady and well balanced, then squat as if sitting until your thighs are just below parallel. The feet should be flat on the floor at all times. Pause at the bottom to eliminate the momentum that can be created by bouncing, and then slowly raise yourself back to the starting position.

Reminder: This is not an arm exercise. Use only the legs and back. Keep your head up at all times by focusing on the point where the ceiling meets the wall. If you're having any trouble with balance, try putting a small board under your heels.

No. 2: Bent-over Rows

Muscles: Latissimus dorsi in the back, the trapezius in the neck, and the deltoids.

Comment: This exercise works the entire shoulder area, the fine muscles of the back, and the broad latissimus muscles that span the back and cover the collarbone. It is the best exercise for the back.

Directions: Stand with your feet comfortably spread. Keeping the legs as straight as possible (knees-locked position), bend over at the waist until your back is parallel with the floor. Take the bar in an overhand grip with the hands slightly wider than shoulder width, and bring the bar off the floor a few inches. (If you have to bend the knees to pick up the bar, that's perfectly all right.) Pull the bar to the chest without moving the upper body. Slowly lower the bar back to the starting position.

Reminder: This exercise is for the back primarily, but obviously the arms get some work as well. Don't let gravity take the bar away from the chest; keep the bar under control.

No. 3: Bench Press

Muscles: Pectorals, shoulders, and triceps.

Comment: This is *the* exercise for the upper body. Since the chest, shoulders, and triceps are all involved, you'll be able to handle quite a bit of weight. It takes a certain amount of skill to raise and lower the weight in the proper form and under control so it may be helpful to practice with a light weight to get the feel of things. If you don't have a weight bench or a suitable substitute, you can do these presses on the floor or on an exercise mat, or do the standing barbell press as described in Chapter 12 instead.

Directions: Pick up the bar with an overhand grip, hands about shoulder width apart or a little wider. Bring the bar to your chest as you did for the squat, slowly sit down on the end of the bench, then lower yourself slowly until your back is flat on the bench and your head is resting comfortably. Keep your feet flat on the floor and slightly spread for leverage. Now press the bar straight up from the chest until your elbows are straight and your arms are fully extended. Pause at the top and lower the bar slowly and carefully until it just touches your chest. If you're using a bench, your elbows will be below the line of the bench in the bottom position. If you're on the floor, your elbows will touch the floor, and the bar may not quite touch your chest.

Reminder: Don't sit too close to the edge of the bench unless it is very stable because it might pop up behind you. Keep your buttocks on the bench at all times and try to arch your back slightly.

No. 4: Curls

Muscles: Biceps and forearms.
Comment: The barbell curl is probably the simplest of the biceps exercises but it produces quick results. And it's still true that people tend to judge muscularity by the size of the biceps.

Directions: Bend over and pick up the bar with an underhand grip, hands a little more than shoulder width apart. Stand up and bring the bar up, using your legs and back until the bar is at arm's length in front of you—about midthigh. Keeping your feet comfortably spread, curl the bar up until it touches your chest. Make sure your back is straight and your head up throughout the exercise. Pause at the top and slowly lower the bar to the midthigh position.

Reminder: Try to keep your style and form during the curls. This means holding the shoulders back and using only the arms for leverage and the elbows as pivots. Lower the bar rather than letting it fall back to the starting position.

No. 5: Triceps Extension

Muscles: Triceps.

Comment: This exercise works directly on the triceps and has very little effect on other muscles except the shoulders. The triceps are underrated, but they play an important role in throwing and swimming, and they give balance to upper-arm strength.

Directions: Bend over, and using an overhand grip, hands about six inches apart, pick up the bar. Your feet should be about shoulder width apart. Stand up with your back straight, or sit straight on a bench. Bring the bar to a position directly over your head; then, using your elbows as pivots, lower the bar slowly behind your head. Keep your upper arms steady and lower the weight as far as you can. Moving only your lower arms, raise the bar back to the overhead position.

Reminder: Keep your back as straight as you can and your head up. This is not an easy exercise, so don't try to use too much weight at first. Try to keep your elbows close to your head throughout the exercise.

No. 6: Stiff-legged Dead Lift

Muscles: Frontal thigh, hamstrings, buttocks, lower back.

Comment: The movements involved in the dead lift provide the best exercise for the lower back, strengthening the muscles and relieving tension at the same time. But this is really a good whole-body exercise as well; it serves to prevent lower back problems, which are the most common medical complaints among athletes and the general public as well.

Directions: Take the same starting position as you did for the bent-over rows. Bend over at the waist, flexing the knees just a little, and grip the bar with an overhand-underhand grip, hands a little wider than shoulder width. Straighten the knees and lift the bar off the floor a few inches.

Keep your back as flat as you can, and keep your head up. Now, keeping your knees straight, stand erect with the bar. Keep arms straight and shoulders back in the standing position. Bend over and lower the weight until it touches the floor.

Reminder: For the most benefit, be sure to exaggerate the shoulder movement when you reach the standing position by thrusting the shoulders back and the chest out. If you need to bend your knees more than suggested, go ahead and do so. You'll eventually be able to do the lift in proper form.

No. 7: Toe Raises

Muscles: Lower leg.

Comment: This is the best and simplest exercise for strengthening the calf muscles. The calves are really quite strong for their size and can take a lot of exercise.

Directions: Stand with your back straight, your head up, and the dumbbells held at your sides, palms in. If you're using the bar, let it hang down in front of you with your arms fully extended. Lock your knees and raise up as high as you can on your toes. Hold at the top for a count of 2 and then slowly lower your heels back to the floor. If you want to increase the stretching motion, stand with your toes on a small block of wood, letting your heels touch the floor.

Reminder: Whether you use a block of wood or not, balance can be a problem with toe raises. With a little practice, however, you'll quickly get the hang of it.

No. 8: Bent-leg Sit-ups

Muscles: Abdominals.

Comment: There are really only two exercises that effectively tighten the stomach: the sit-up and the leg raise. I prefer the sit-up because it seems to concentrate more intensely on the lower abdomen.

Directions: Lie flat on your back on the floor and flex your knees until your feet also are flat on the floor. Hook your toes under a barbell, a bed, or anything that will hold them firmly. Put your hands behind your head. Next, curl your body up from the waist until your elbows touch your knees, and then lower yourself back to the starting position. Pause for a count of 2 and repeat.

Start with 10 repetitions and add one sit-up every other day. When you can do just about as many sit-ups as you want without getting sore stomach muscles, you can increase the intensity of the exercise by holding a light dumbbell behind your head.

Reminder: This is a stomach exercise, so if you feel any strain in your legs or back, increase your concentration and make sure the abdomen is getting the work. Don't bounce up from the floor because it will be momentum doing the work, not you.

If you continue to increase resistance and the number of sets (up to three) as you get stronger, these eight exercises are really all you'll ever need to build muscle and maintain a high level of fitness. As you can see, the exercises work the entire body, all the major muscle groups, and many of the minor muscles as well—neck, upper back, shoulders, lower back, chest, biceps, triceps, buttocks, front thigh, hamstrings, calves, and abdomen. Four of the exercises work the legs; there are three for the back, three for the arms, two for the shoulders, and one each for the chest, buttocks, and stomach.

I suggest that you stick with one set of each exercise for at least twelve workouts; that's a month's worth of work if you maintain the schedule of three workouts a week. At that point you will be much better equipped to estimate and chart your progress. You may want to move up to two sets at that time or stay at one set, but increase the amount of weight you're using for each exercise. You may want to add some of the exercises described in the next chapter, or substitute some of them for the Basic Eight. These decisions will come naturally, and I'm sure you'll want continually to test yourself and experiment with new combinations.

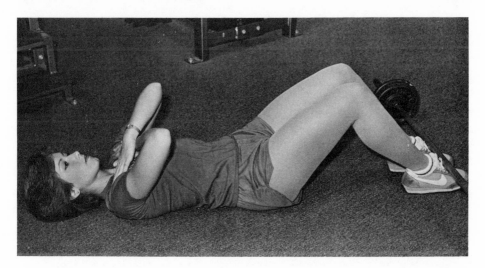

Variety is important because it's very easy to get bored and go stale if you continue exactly the same routine month in and month out. But regardless of the combination you use, I know you will see progress in as little as one month, and that should be motivation enough.

·||| Chapter 13 |||·

PLUS TEN

As I said, the Basic Eight exercises in the previous chapter are remarkably good for working the entire body, but there are actually dozens of more specific exercises that you can add to them, exercises that will work directly on the biceps, triceps, deltoids, and so on. I've selected ten additional exercises that will be of particular benefit to people who get serious about weight training, but will also be useful to those of you who are only lifting to enhance your total physical condition.

If your goal is total fitness, which includes cardiovascular fitness, then the amount of the weight you use for each exercise will slowly increase and the amount of rest time between exercises will decrease. This will maintain your high pulse rate and stimulate muscular growth at the same time. These additional exercises can be added over time as your level of fitness continues to improve. Obviously, everyone's progress will be different, so let your body dictate its own needs and abilities.

The additional exercises described here are divided by body part so that you can easily select the specific exercises you want to add to your routine.

FOR THE CHEST

Dumbbell Flys. Take a dumbbell in each hand and lie down on a bench (or the floor). Your back should be flat. Bring the dumbbells together over your chest (palms facing). Your arms should be almost fully extended, with just a slight angle at the elbow. Lower the weight slowly to the sides until your arms are parallel with the floor. Return to the starting position.

94

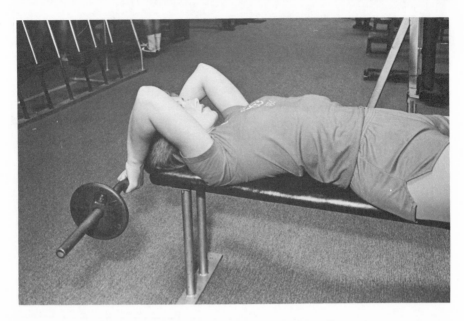

Bent-arm Pullovers. Lie on the bench (or the floor) with the barbell behind your head. Grasp the barbell with an overhand grip, keeping the elbows bent and close to the ears in the same way you did for the triceps extensions. Keep the elbows bent and raise the weight from the floor until the weight is over the chest. Return to the starting position and repeat.

FOR THE SHOULDERS

Press Behind the Neck. Stand with the feet about shoulder width apart and place the bar on your shoulders as you did for the squats. Your elbows should be pointing directly out to the sides. Press the weight slowly over your head, pause at the top, and lower slowly. Keep your head up and your back straight throughout the exercise.

Upright Rows. Stand straight, feet comfortably spread, head up, and the bar at arm's length across your thighs. Lift the bar along the plane of your body until the bar is just under the chin. Pause for a count of 1 and lower the bar slowly to the starting position.

FOR THE ARMS

Alternate Dumbbell Presses. Take a dumbbell in each hand and raise them to your shoulders, palms facing in. Stand with your back straight and your feet comfortably spread. Now press one dumbbell straight up until your elbow is locked. Lower it slowly and as you do, begin to raise the other dumbbell. Continue to alternate.

Dips. Use either parallel bars or two sturdy chairs for this exercise. With your arms at your sides, support your body in the suspended position. If you're using chairs, you'll have to curl your legs up under you. Lower yourself as far as you can by allowing your elbows to bend, then press back up to the starting position.

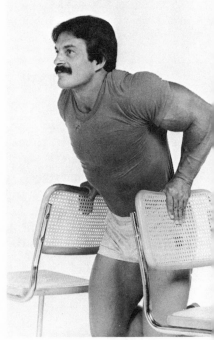

FOR THE LEGS

Lunges. Place the bar on your shoulders, keeping your back straight and head up. Lunge forward with the right leg and plant your foot on the floor about two feet in front of you. Let your back heel come off the floor and lower your knee as far as you can, touching the floor if possible. Hold for a count of 2 and then push back to the starting position. Repeat with the other leg.

FOR THE BACK

Good Mornings. Place the bar on your shoulders as you did for the lunges and spread your feet slightly wider than shoulder width. Keep your legs straight and bend over at the waist until your chest is parallel with the floor. Keep your back straight and your head up at all times. Return to the starting position.

Dumbbell Swing. Stand with your feet spread widely and a lightweight dumbbell held directly over your head with both hands. Slowly swing the dumbbell in an arc as far as you can through your legs. Keep the weight under control as you retrace the arc back to the starting position.

FOR THE ABDOMEN

Leg Raises. Lie flat on the floor with your legs together and your arms at your sides. Slowly raise both legs together, keeping your knees locked. Raise the legs until they are perpendicular with the floor. Lower slowly until the heels are a couple of inches off the floor and repeat.

That completes the entire routine, eighteen exercises in all. If you decide at some point in your development to do all of them, allow at least an hour to complete three sets of 6 to 10 repetitions.

·||| Chapter 14 |||·

WEIGHT TRAINING
FOR WOMEN

The question arrives on a tidal wave of controversy: Should women lift weights to develop and strengthen their bodies? The women's movement and consciousness-raising efforts in general have had considerable success in challenging the issues surrounding male and female role distinctions and expectations. But the next step, leading to the rethinking of body images, has met with considerable resistance.

Our collective consciousnesses have been duly raised. We have come a long way and now accept most newly defined social roles. In spite of the advances women have made in the social and economic realms, women who appear physically confident and competent still threaten everyone—both men and other women. Notions of what is physically acceptable for each gender, especially the female, are apparently rigid and deep-seated. Though it is true that men have altered their concepts of the physical ideal somewhat, the departure from what has traditionally been considered the norm of male sexuality hasn't been all that dramatic. The masculine ideal has always been to be muscular and physically fit. Underlying the resistance to alteration of women's physical image is a certain feminine mystique—the idea that women are the weaker sex and that sports and heavy exertion are unladylike.

Cathy Gelfo, chairwoman of the International Federation of Bodybuilders Women's Physique Committee, author of *Heavy Duty Training for Women,* and a body-builder herself, views the situation this way: "Women have always been confined to a small number of socially acceptable roles. Traditionally, being strong and fit has not been included. The right to a healthy and strong body has been denied to us by our sex."

Despite the resistance that will always exist to a certain extent, all indexes point to the fact that women are passionately involved in fashioning a new physical image and new physical ideals for themselves. Call a woman of the 1980s a member of the "weaker sex" and you risk getting the boom lowered. Women have taken the first step toward awareness in recognizing their potential as action-oriented people. Coupled with this recognition is a growing security that allows women to throw out the old concepts and assume the responsibility of defining themselves. For many, the notion of an improved and stronger physical self actually precedes the fact of such change. It has been widely known for a long time, well before anthropologist Ashley Montagu courageously stated it, that despite certain physical inferiorities, women are psychologically and emotionally tougher, more constant and enduring than men.

Today's woman, with full awareness of her emotional and mental strength, wants a body and a physical image that is more consistent with that stronger self-image. In an informal survey I asked twenty-five women body-builders of various ages and experience about their prime motivation for training. "Feeling better about myself" was the answer most often given. Several psychological studies of female athletes at the high-school and college levels compared them to nonathletes. The athletes proved to be less dependent on the opinions of others, to have a higher sense of self-esteem and improvement, and to have a generally healthier philosophy of life.

The comments of the respondents to my tiny survey did suggest that the process of altering their bodies through training and dieting, and the subsequent visible improvement, were instrumental in strengthening self-image and enhancing confidence. Susan Frye, assistant editor of *Shape*, the largest of the new magazines on women's body-building, says, "The improvements I saw in my body as the result of Nautilus training—mainly better tone and muscle definition—definitely benefited my self-image and it goes without saying that a stronger sense of self-esteem increases one's confidence in all interpersonal relations, including sex." This kind of comment reveals a growing awareness among women that their physical image makes a social statement, and many are making this statement consciously and assertively.

Viewed within the traditional framework of social values, a woman pursuing a career in athletics is pursuing a male role. In her book *The*

Psychology of Sport, Dorcas Susan Butt comments on such role conflict by saying, "The role of athlete and the role of female are opposed. The aggressiveness, strength, competitiveness, and independence of the male athlete are in sharp contrast to the gentle submission, sensitivity, weakness, and dependence described for the female position."

Confronted with prejudices about role expectations that are deeply entrenched, it's natural for even the emotionally strong woman athlete to harbor some concern about her femininity. It is even harder for the average women to take up a sport like weight lifting, with its overwhelming masculine connotations. The female body-builder carries a double burden when facing ingrained cultural prejudices, as her physical image along with her behavior, is cause for question. A top professional female body-builder, Stacey Bentley, winner of the prestigious 1980 Zane Invitational award and other top titles, worried about her femininity when she took to body-building. She comments on her evolving attitude regarding her body-building activities: "My big concern when I started working out was that I might become too manly. My concern about appearing masculine disappeared, however, when I entered my first competition. My body was then very defined and I saw and felt my muscles directly under my skin. I thought to myself that I'm not overly massive but I sure am beautiful."

"Let's be honest," I went on, "there are a lot of women who don't find our bodies particularly attractive and wouldn't want to marry us either."

The majority of men still find it difficult to view women as anything but sex objects. This may be due in part to the *Playboy* philosophy, which has become part of the masculine ideal of woman. Body-building and physique posing may offer one of the few alternatives for sexual display open to women with a desire and need to express themselves physically.

SHAPING UP WITH WEIGHT TRAINING

Most women still think pumping iron will give them large, unfeminine muscles. Less than 1 percent of the male population has the capacity to develop a massive size, and likewise 99 percent of women couldn't develop a body like Ms. America Laura Coombes', even if they wanted to. The reason men are bigger and stronger than women is because of the male hormone testosterone, which operates on the growth mechanism of the male body. The small percentage of women who have large muscles have either inherited a genetic predisposition toward muscle mass or have an unusually high quantity of testosterone in their system.

While the adrenal and sex glands of women do secrete a small amount of testosterone, it isn't enough to provide for much in the way of muscular development. The truth is, even though the majority of women couldn't develop large muscles if their lives depended on it, every woman can benefit from vigorous, intense weight training.

While the typical man's body weight is approximately 15 percent fat, the typical women's body is 25 percent fat. This difference in body fat levels is due, in part, to the fact that female hormones—especially estrogen—promote fat. It's also true, however, that women traditionally have been discouraged from participating in athletics and exerting themselves vigorously. As a result, most women have never developed much strength or muscle tone.

The bodies of sedentary people continue to change composition as they grow older, primarily with the addition of fat. This means that more of the total body weight will be fatty tissue and less will be lean body mass or muscle tissue. The loss of muscle tissue makes it more and more difficult to lose fat, and this results in a cycle that is hard to change, especially for women. Men have more lean body mass and less fat to start with because of a higher basal metabolic rate (BMR), anywhere from 5 percent to 20 percent higher than women.

Some of the male's leanness may be a sexual characteristic, but it is leaner people of either sex who have a higher BMR. This greater leanness means an ability to accommodate greater caloric intake without fattening, and it also facilitates the burning of fat. Muscle tissue is much more active than fat tissue. Muscle burns more calories even at rest. So while low-calorie diets may result in weight loss, they are more effective when combined with exercise that strengthens and tones muscle. Studies have revealed that 25 to 90 percent of the weight loss resulting from dietary restriction alone comes from muscle, organs, and fluid and not from fat. This loss of protein from muscles and organs is difficult to prevent even with a small caloric reduction in an inactive person and explains the wrinkling and sagging tissues that so often accompany weight loss by diet.

For some, increased activity alone will turn the tide. One study found that overweight college women lost an average of 5.3 pounds in a two-month period during which they participated in a four-day-a-week, one-hour-per-session exercise program without any dietary restrictions. Skinfold measurements revealed that the weight loss was the result of a much larger loss of fatty tissue with a gain in muscle.

Obviously then, the procedure for promoting weight loss and altering body composition for improved appearance is a combination of diet and intense physical exercise.

ASSESSING YOURSELF

Of all the reasons women list for taking up an exercise and diet program, increasing sex appeal is still uppermost in the minds of a great majority. After all, vanity is a strong motivator for most of us. In a world where you present yourself to others daily, looking good is of paramount importance.

The woman who has been sedentary for any length of time need not be reminded she is losing her shape. There are certain areas that sag, dimple, and expand, serving as stark visible reminders of physical deterioration and declining sex appeal. More often than not, the encroachment of the cellulite look and sagging tissues is due to poor muscle tone that results from insufficient exercise. Proper exercise then is part of the answer to regaining youthful form. Here are three trouble spots women need to watch, and exercises that will help firm them.

THE WAISTLINE

In his book, *Sun and Steel,* which described his own physical transformation from a thick, overly ripe intellectual into a well-developed body-builder, the late Japanese author Yukio Mishima had this to say about one aspect of physical deterioration with which we can all identify: "I had always felt such signs of physical individuality as a bulging belly (sign of spiritual sloth) to be excessively ugly. To me, this could only be seen as an act of shameless indecency, as though the owner were exposing his or her spiritual pudenda on the outside of his or her body."

Nothing seems to make a woman more painfully aware of her physical deterioration than a bulging waistline. The first requisite in waist reduction is the elimination of excess fat and bloat. Reducing the fatty tissue circling the waist will come only from a reduction in the percentage of fat in the body. This is done most safely and effectively by reducing daily calorie intake while at the same time eating a well-balanced diet. Reducing calories below maintenance levels will result in fat loss over the entire body. If you're persistent with your diet, you'll ultimately see a dramatic reduction in the fat around your waist. But keep in mind that fat used for energy while on a diet comes fairly uniformly from the body's multiple fat stores, never from an isolated area like the waistline. Since that loss is a relatively slow process, it will take a while before significant results are seen. The degree to which you reduce daily caloric intake can be varied according to individual needs, but a minimum reduction of five hundred calories per day is necessary to stimulate real loss. On the other hand, it's unwise for nutritional reasons to reduce intake to less than twelve hundred calories per day.

Exercise

While your diet is cutting into that unsightly flab, exercise will be essential for the improvement of muscle tone and will tighten the whole midsection. Exercise, of course, raises your activity quotient and metabolic rate so that some body fat is used for energy.

It's a natural tendency to perform extra repetitions when training the abdomen, thinking that spot reduction is possible. It isn't. Fat is general, and spot reduction is a myth. Fat cannot be burned off one particular area of the body and that area only.

Intensive physical conditioning exercises can cause a depletion in fat deposits and an increase in lean body weight. In fact, it's possible to maintain the same weight but change body composition with a decrease in body fat and a balancing increase in muscular tissue.

A 1975 issue of the *Physical Fitness Research Digest* concluded, "It is possible to increase caloric expenditure sufficiently by means of regular exercise alone to produce a marked decrease in fat. However, exercise combined with dietary regulation is the more desirable approach to fat reduction."

The same issue also reported, "Intensive weight training programs result in desirable changes of body composition in six to ten weeks of time. These changes are reflected in skinfold reductions, in decreases in absolute and relative fat, in increases in arm, shoulder and chest girths, and in increased lean body weight."

Remember, though, regardless of changes in body composition and fat reduction that result from increased energy expenditure, the waist will trim down only in direct proportion to the loss of overall body fat.

Exercises for the Waist

The following exercises also help the waist. Two groups of muscles are directly involved—the trunk flexors and the hip flexors. The trunk flexors are those muscles in the abdominal cavity with attachments to the ribs, pelvis, and spine. The hip flexors are muscles that cross the hip joint and have attachments to the femur, pelvis, and lower spine.

These five exercises take only minutes a day and work all the muscles of the waist and abdomen evenly. They will bring remarkable results if performed at least four times a week.

No. 1: Lying Leg Raise Lie on a bench (or the floor) with your buttocks on the edge of the bench and your legs hanging over. Use your hands for balance behind you and raise your feet, with your knees slightly bent, to a position just short of perpendicular. Pause a moment and lower your legs until your heels are just above the floor. Repeat 10 times and increase 1 a day up to 50.

No. 2: Sitting Leg Tuck This is a more difficult variation of the leg raise which you can use as your condition improves. Sit on the floor with your hands behind you. Stretch your legs, point your toes, and raise your feet just off the ground. Bend your knees and try to touch them to your chin. Then extend your legs up to a 45-degree angle to the body. Lower your legs slowly to the starting position. Repeat 10 times and add 1 every other day up to 30.

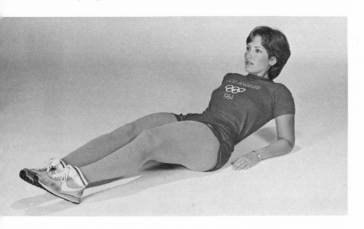

No. 3: Bent-knees Sit-up Lie on your back, bend your knees, and put your feet under a stationary object. Cross your arms on your chest and sit up until your hands touch your knees; pause and lower slowly. Repeat 10 times, adding 1 a day up to 50. If you've been inactive for so long that 10 bent knees sit-ups are too hard, don't worry because there is an alternative that will quickly build abdominal strength and you'll soon be able to do the bent-knees sit-up. It's the following exercise.

No. 4: Negative Accentuated Sit-up Start in the same position for the bent-knees sit-up. This time begin at the top and lower the body to the floor very slowly; take 4 to 8 seconds. Use your arms to get back to the starting position. Repeat 10 times. After a couple of weeks try the original sit-up and it will be much easier.

No. 5: Side Bend Stand with the feet about shoulder width apart. Clasp your hands behind your head. Keep your legs straight and bend slowly to the left as far as possible without leaning forward or backward. Return to the starting position and bend to the right. This will tighten the sides of the waist by alternately stretching and contracting the muscles. Repeat 10 times to each side and add 2 a day up to 50.

Each set of each exercise should be performed for 10 reps at the beginning. At each subsequent training session add 1 or 2 reps, depending on how you feel and your rate of improvement. When you can do 15 to 20 reps rather easily, increase the resistance by performing the exercises more slowly. When you reach the point where you can do 15 to 20 reps in the slow manner, you're ready for even more resistance, and this resistance can be provided by small objects—2½- to 5-pound barbell plates, for example. When performing the leg raises or knee tuck, hold the small plate between your feet or have someone provide manual resistance by pressing down on your legs as you raise and lower them. For the sit-up, hold the plate on your chest. For side bends, hold the plate in your hands behind your head.

A tight midsection, with firm, defined muscles, is a readily attainable goal for the average woman. Whatever your present condition, start and don't be discouraged. The combination of diet and exercise—if you are faithful to them—will soon create a healthier and more shapely appearance.

SHAPING THE BUTTOCKS

A bulging belly may be the first warning signal telling a woman it's time to shape up, but since people rarely get a good view of their backsides, it's easy to be unaware that the posterior is even farther gone than the midsection. Because of the woman's naturally larger and broader pelvic girdle, as well as the hormonal predisposition to fat buildup in the hips and buttocks, the dimpled buttocks will usually give an even clearer indication, at least to others, of a lack of condition. And the problem with the buttocks is that you can diet like a Spartan with little visible improvement.

The reason diet alone can't help is that a sagging and deteriorating derrière is the result of diminished muscle tone in the gluteus muscles of the buttocks. While little can be done to change the shape of the bosom, there is always hope for the "glutes," the name body-builders use in referring to the buttocks. It's possible to train away that so-called cellulite, and get rid of the dimples, pockmarks, and ripples that plague many women. A program of persistent, intense exercise will do the job. Combined with a sensible diet, exercise can streamline the buttocks.

Exercises for the Buttocks

It is properly toned muscle tissue that gives people shape and form. Fat has no tone or firmness at all. Since the buttocks problem is due to loss of muscle tissue itself, the only solution is to strengthen the entire area, including the gluteus muscles, rear thighs, and lower back. High-repetition flexibility exercises, like those often seen in women's magazines, will do little to help because the intensity of effort required is just too low.

Progressive resistance exercises provided by barbells or Nautilus equipment is required to develop and tighten the glutes. With progressive resistance, all that is needed is one set of 8 to 12 reps of three exercises. For optimal results the intensity of the exercise must be high. This can be assured if your last rep is hard to perform. No, it's not the easiest form of exercise. And yes, it requires effort. But it is the only type that produces any worthwhile results.

No. 1: Squats These are probably the best exercises for working the hips, buttocks, and thighs. Place a bar across your upper back. With your back as straight as a ramrod and your head looking up, squat down until your thighs are slightly below parallel with the floor. Without pausing, return to the starting position, always keeping a straight back.

No. 2: Dead Lifts With your ankles against the bar, knees slightly bent, and head looking up, grasp the bar with an overhand grip and stand erect with the bar straight down at arm's length. Pause momentarily and lower the bar slowly back to the floor. This exercise works the entire back side of the body from head to toe and will do wonders for tightening the problem area.

No. 3: Lunges These can be done with dumbbells or barbells. Holding a bar across your upper back, stride forward with your left foot and then push yourself all the way back to the starting position in one step. Repeat with the right leg. If using dumbbells, hold them at arm's length at your side and do the same thing. Lunges exercise the hips and buttocks.

Perform these three exercises every other day. Do 8 reps for each. The last rep shouldn't be easy. When the weight you use allows for 12 reps, add 5 percent more weight and reduce the reps back to 8. This is the nature of progressive resistance exercises. These exercises make good use of the simplest and most widely available pieces of resistance equipment known—the plate-loading barbell and the dumbbell.

More productive than conventional equipment, and my personal preference, are the Nautilus machines mentioned elsewhere in this book. If you belong to a gym with Nautilus, you'll find these two exercises particularly effective.

No. 4: The Geared Hip and Back Machine The first step is getting into the starting position. This is accomplished by adjusting the shoulder pads, buckling the retaining belt, and cranking yourself into place. Next, extend the legs by pushing against the padded movement arms behind the knees. The extension of the upper thighs provides direct resistance to the buttocks as well as the lower back.

If you were allowed only one exercise for shaping the buttocks, this machine would be the best bet. It is the single most productive exercise for the hips and buttocks.

No. 5: Leg-curl Machine Lying on your stomach, position yourself so that your Achilles tendons make contact with the padded movement arm. Under control, curl the lower leg until the pad hits the buttocks. Pause and lower slowly.

SHAPING THE BUST

Of all of women's physical and sexual attributes, the highest premium in our society is placed on the bustline. Studies by psychologists reveal that 95 percent of adult females are unhappy with their breast development. Women who feel they have been shortchanged desire a more shapely, fuller bustline, while those with larger breasts worry about lack of firmness and sagging. Testimony to women's preoccupation with the appearance of their bustline is the lucrative business that has responded to their "needs." Gimmicks of all sorts can be found at the back of most women's magazines. There are exercises that promise added inches, and creams and massage treatments that are said to stimulate growth.

Forget these gimmicks, be realistic, and be prepared to spend a little time on yourself. First, you have to accept the fact that the size and shape of your bust are inherited features and are not subject to dramatic alteration. Very little can be done to change the size and shape of the bust outside of drug treatments, surgery, silicone injections, or a large increase or decrease in body fat. Then decide you'll bring your bust up to its potential. That, of course, means exercise. Before beginning this chest program, it's wise to do two warm-up movements. Don't rest or cool down between the warm-ups and the exercises.

Exercises for the Bust

Warm-up No. 1: Arm Circles Stand erect with your arms held
horizontally. Without bending your elbows, make a twelve-inch circle
with your hands. Go in one direction 16 times and then reverse and do 15
in the other direction.

Warm-up No. 2: Push-ups with Knees Bent Get on your hands and knees on the floor. With knees bent and hands directly beneath the shoulders, push up. Do 1 set of 10 reps.

No. 1: Dumbbell Flys Lie on your back on a bench (or the floor) with your feet firmly on the floor. Hold a dumbbell in each hand with arms extended straight up over your face. With a slight bend in elbows, lower your arms to the sides. Return to the starting position. Repeat.

No. 2: Barbell or Dumbbell Bench Press Press up from the chest in a straight line. Control is important; move slowly and deliberately.

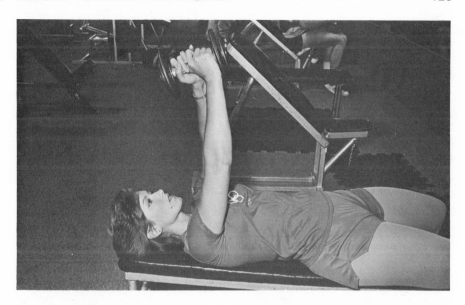

No. 3: Flat Pullover Lie on your back, feet on the floor. Use one dumbbell, holding it straight-arm over your head. Lower the dumbbell as far back as possible behind your head. Return to the starting position.

These exercises should be repeated three days a week. Use a weight that allows 8 reps in good style at the beginning. As you progress, increase resistance slowly.

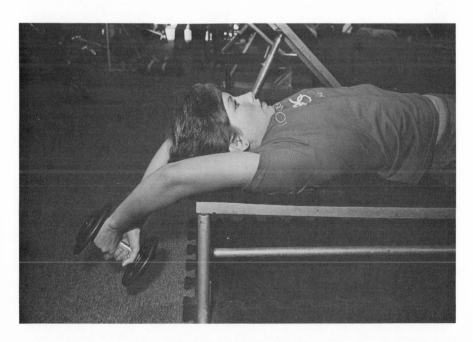

If you train in a Nautilus gym, substitute the following exercises.

No. 4: Pullover Machine Sit erect, fasten the seat belt, and push on the foot pedal. This moves the elbow pads into position to get the upper arms on the pads. Allow the upper arms to be stretched behind as far as comfortable. Then press the pads and move the elbows to a position behind the torso.

No. 5: Double Chest Machine Two exercises are involved here. The first is done in an alternate-arm fashion. The right arm pushes against the elbow pad as the movement arm rotates to the position shown in the first photo. As the right arm returns, the left arm is moved in a similar fashion. Direct resistance is provided for the large muscles that lie across the front of the chest without tiring your arm muscles.

The second exercise is done immediately after the first. The starting position is shown in the second photo. The parallel bars are pushed forward until your arms are straight. This allows you to use the muscles of your arms to force your exhausted chest muscles to work even harder.

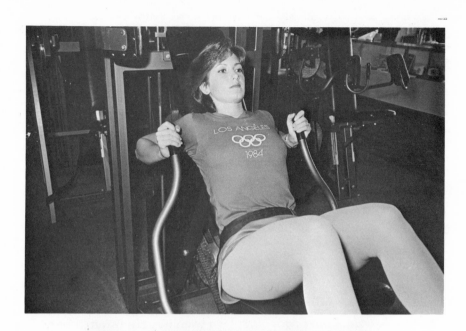

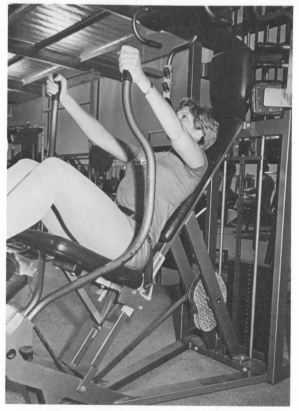

Stacey Bentley

Though I'm loath to say it, I have to admit I was indifferent to the idea of women's body-building when it first made headlines about four years ago. It wasn't that women with well-developed bodies offended my view of what femininity was supposedly about, it was just that I didn't think a woman could develop enough muscle mass or definition to warrant my critical attention as a body-builder. Some of the first women's body-building contests held in 1977 and 1978 served only to reaffirm my indifference. The winners of those early competitions won because of their ample feminine attributes, not because of muscle development.

I simply couldn't understand why these contests were referred to as body-building competitions when they were more like traditional beauty contests, the winner having the most sexually appealing body, not the best-developed athletic body. Fearful that the public would not accept a body-building contest for women, the promoters and officials of those first contests opted in favor of those bodies which were more in line with traditional tastes.

The real athletes who sweated and toiled in the gym and suffered the privations of severe dieting, simply were not rewarded for their efforts. Fortunately, there were women who remained loyal and true to their goals despite competitive setbacks. It was women like Laura Coombes, Claudia

Stacey Bentley

Wilbourn, Stacey Bentley, and Rachael McLish who had the courage of their convictions. They continued heavy training to develop their bodies further, and they finally changed attitudes about the physical potential of women.

Laura Coombes was the first to open my eyes. I was the guest poser at the 1980 Florida State Men's and Women's Body-building Championships and was asked to be a judge for the women's event. Not knowing what to expect, I settled back comfortably in my seat, anticipating little excitement. When the competitors filed onstage, the first thing I noticed was that none of them wore the high heels or one-piece bathing suits that are standard at traditional beauty contests. All were barefooted and wore tasteful but brief bikinis so the judges could get a better view of their abdominal definition and lower-back development.

Once all the women had made their entrance and the lineup was complete, my eyes settled immediately on Laura Coombes of Tallahassee, Florida. Never in my wildest dreams could I conjure the image of a woman with such extreme muscular detail and development. While there were several other women who had obviously done a lot of work—all possessing rippling abdominals, bulging biceps, and looking simply incredible—Laura just had too much of everything.

I sat through the remainder of the prejudging, my mouth hanging open incredulously as these female athletes routed me from my indifference. The competition was capped by Coombes' free-posing performance, which had the audience on its feet. Just as she had done several times before, but without success, Laura let loose with a battery of muscular poses usually associated with male body-builders and shunned by the traditional school of women's body-building. This time, however, Laura was named the 1980 Florida women's champion.

In the summer of 1980, Laura, at twenty-six, won the first American Women's Body-building Championship and established a new and higher physical standard by which women physique competitors will be measured in the future.

To ensure that women's competitions continue to move in this positive direction, Ben Weider, president of the International Federation of Body-builders (IFBB), the officially recognized, sanctioning organization for all body-building contests worldwide, formed a Women's Physique Committee at the 1979 IFBB Congress in Columbus, Ohio. The members of that committee set down rules and guidelines for judging women that are similar to those used for men's contests. The women will be scrutinized through three rounds of judging. In the first round the relaxed

Laura Coombes

views are from the left, right, front, and back, with the arms at the sides. In the second round there are six compulsory poses designed to exhibit all the body's skeletal muscles from the front, sides, and back. The third round gives each competitor one minute to perform her own posing routine to music. This is probably the most visually exciting because it's highly creative and shows the body to its best advantage.

The recent surge of interest in women's body-building has resulted in an increase in the number of competitions available. The Amateur Athletic Union (AAU) has information about all local, state, or national contests.

PREPARING FOR WOMEN'S COMPETITION

Before Coombes' decisive victory in the 1980 championships, women who wanted to compete successfully were confused about how to proceed with their training because there were no formalized judging standards. If they trained too intensely and developed appreciable muscle mass and dieted for too long and became extremely defined, they might offend the traditionalists. But then, after all, it was a body-building contest and, theoretically, the best-conditioned body would win. Now, however, the most developed and shapely muscles, devoid of all traces of body fat, will win, just as in men's competitions. And though it is highly unlikely we will ever see a female body-builder develop musculature similar to that of a top male (even Coombes at her biggest and best is diminutive compared to the top men), the training regime and dieting practices of the female competitors should be approximately the same as the males'. Any woman who wishes to develop her muscles to their fullest potential will have to train very intensely. The physiology of muscle growth is essentially the same for both sexes, and because it is the intensity of effort as opposed to the duration that is responsible for muscle growth, both sexes must train as intensely as possible when seeking rapid and large-scale increases in muscle mass.

And because the laws of nutrition apply equally to women, they will have to consume well-balanced but reduced-calorie diets prior to competition so they can maintain their mass while reducing fat.

A CHAMPION PREPARES

It was during the prejudging of the first Ms. Olympia Contest in Philadelphia in August 1980 that I discovered the perfect answer for those critics of women body-builders who say that musclewomen are less feminine than other women—her name is Rachael McLish of Harlingen,

Texas. Her competitive career has been short but spectacular. In 1978, McLish won her first amateur contest, the U.S. Women's Championships, in Atlantic City. And in 1980 she won the Ms. Olympia, the most prestigious of all. Her physique, perhaps more than that of any other female competitor, has an appeal that extends beyond the body-building subculture to the culture at large. Combining sizable muscular mass with extreme definition and perfect proportions, she has retained a feminine grace that has universal appeal.

The following workout routine is typical of the type used by Rachael McLish and Laura Coombes. It's obviously more advanced than those in the previous chapter, but it is very much in line with the routines used by top male body-builders. In fact, the only difference would be in the amount of weight used for each exercise. Generally two sets of six to eight repetitions with one or two forced repetitions at the end of each set comprise a complete workout for a muscle group. This particular sequence is designed to be used four days a week—Monday, Tuesday, Thursday, and Friday—with the chest and back worked on two days and the arms, legs, and abdomen the other two days. Descriptions of most of these exercises will be found in other chapters.

On Monday and Thursday:

Rachael McLish

Chest. One cycle of Nautilus chest and seated bench presses; dumbbell flys on the flat bench, incline and decline benches; and cable crossovers.

Back. Seated rows; lateral pull-downs, one-arm lateral pulldowns; one-arm dumbbell rows.

On Tuesday and Friday:

Arms. Biceps: Concentration curls; Nautilus curl machine; standing cable curls. Triceps: Triceps presses, dips, dumbbell French presses. Shoulders: Lateral raises, dumbbell presses, upright and bent-over rows. Trapezius: Shrugs.

Legs. One cycle of leg extensions and leg presses; squats; leg curls; toe raises.

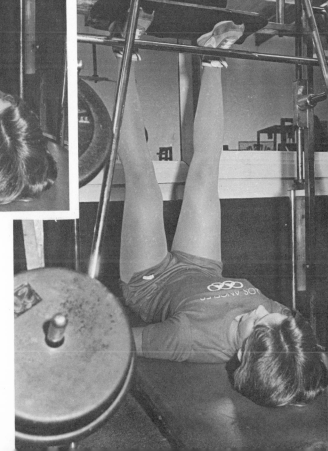

Abdomen. Decline sit-ups with weight (3 sets of 25); crunches (3 sets of 25); leg raises (3 sets of 25).

Competitive women body-builders also diet during training and especially before contests. A typical diet during training would include a well-balanced menu, with no special emphasis on protein consumption. If there is a need to build muscle, more calories than normal will be required. Whole grains, fruits and vegetables, fish, chicken, and low-fat cheeses are important in this kind of diet, and one must make a conscious effort to stay away from junk foods, processed foods, and sugar. An occasional fling with high-calorie or high-fat foods is all right.

Two or three weeks before a contest, calories have to be cut back, and this means more raw vegetables and fruit with the addition of lean meat for protein. Definition can be increased during this intense training period by increasing aerobic exercise—running, biking, skipping rope.

It's important to remember that most women simply will not develop muscular mass whatever they do, but that lack of bulk doesn't mean that strength and definition are not improving. And don't forget the other advantages of weight training—reduced body fat levels, improved endurance, and a self-image second to none.

·||| Chapter 15 |||·

TEENAGERS

I first got interested in body-building at the age of twelve. It happened by accident, really. I was in the neighborhood drugstore in my hometown of Ephrata, Pennsylvania, just leafing through the magazines when the cover of one of the popular muscle magazines of that time caught my eye. Looking back on it, I think I knew at that very moment that I wanted to be a champion body-builder. The pictures of all those bulging muscles were definitely awe-inspiring and a bit intimidating, but I decided to find out more about body-building and to get some of those barbells I saw in the magazine ads.

I couldn't wait to get home and tell my parents about this wonderful discovery and I was shocked when they didn't quite share my enthusiasm for the idea. Nevertheless, I did get a set of barbells that Christmas and a small booklet that outlined a dozen or so exercises that were "absolutely guaranteed" to give me a massive physique. One of the best moves I ever made was following that rather simplistic book very faithfully. It wasn't the exercises themselves that were so valuable but the advice that the beginner—or the advanced weight trainer, for that matter—should work out only three times a week, and never more than two hours at a time.

Any weight trainer will tell you, especially the young and enthusiastic beginner, that the desire to build muscle quickly far exceeds the body's capacity to handle the stress. Intense daily workouts that follow that initial love affair with the weights do more to tear you down than to build you up. The body needs recovery time; growth has to be gradual. The fatigue and soreness that go along with crash programs serve only to slow progress and destroy motivation.

In reality, I was probably a little young when I started working out. The muscles of a preadolescent don't respond as quickly or as extensively to resistance training as they do after puberty. But whether I was really gaining muscle or not, I was gaining a completely new perspective on myself and a respect for my body and its capabilities that I had never had before. I developed a strong self-image and had the courage to stand up to my classmates who wanted me to try out for team sports. I somehow knew that if I really was going to develop my body I wouldn't have time to spend training seriously for other sports.

A lot of people, including my family and friends, thought the idea of closing yourself up in a room and fiddling with weights was a bit strange, but that didn't bother me. Weight lifting is naturally a rather solitary sport, even at the gym. Nobody really helps you, and I quickly learned that the advice being dispensed by other body-builders there was a lot less valuable than my own instincts. So I kept at it, following my little book. I found that there wasn't any good advice available from the coaches at my school either, because they didn't believe in the benefits of weight training, knew very little about it, and, therefore, couldn't be very helpful except to warn about stunting my growth, becoming musclebound, and hurting my back. Later I learned for myself that the lower back is one of the weakest parts of the young body, but negative advice from adults who didn't really care didn't slow me up.

Since that time, of course, weight training has become almost universally accepted as an effective, efficient method of developing strength, power, endurance, and flexibility; performed rhythmically and consecutively with only brief rests between sets, it develops the cardiovascular system.

Today, school authorities at all levels are better informed and aware that a carefully chosen weight-training routine that lasts several months can:

- Improve overall physical condition

- Improve posture

- Enhance appearance

- Bring a change in body composition

- Change body shape and measurements

- Control weight

- Encourage self-discipline

- Create self-confidence

Some of the most dramatic changes I've seen have taken place in young people who are not well-developed physically and have always thought of themselves as small and weak. Weight training is so easily adaptable to individual capabilities that even the smallest youngsters can make visible improvements in a very short time, improvements that will motivate them to continue at even a higher level of commitment.

Studies conducted by private and governmental researchers have documented the relative upper-body weakness of young girls and women, particularly in the arms and shoulders. The Mentzer Method also works for teenage girls. In fact, weight training is fast becoming a popular fitness activity for girls.

And part of the reason for the new popularity of weight training for women and girls is the realization that these exercises don't develop bulky, mannish muscles but just the opposite—a trim, well-shaped figure.

One of the real beauties of weight training is that the selection of exercises, the weight used, and the number of sets and repetitions are easily tailored to the capacity, objectives, and needs of the individual.

I fully realize that most junior high schools and many high schools still don't have weight-training programs, facilities, or trained adult supervision, but that doesn't mean that weight lifting can't become as much a part of a fitness program for teenagers as running, wrestling, tennis, or the organized team sports. This lagging interest in schools may mean you'll have to pursue your weight training at home, in a "Y," or at a private health club, where the instruction may range from good to nonexistent.

But regardless of the availability of formal instruction, teenagers can become weight trainers by following the program described in this chapter and in Chapters 12 and 13. As I've said before, the first necessity—for everyone—is goal setting and understanding that the young body, as strong as it may be, is not going to develop bulky muscles quickly. Twelve- to fifteen-year-olds will not get results as quickly as youngsters who are sixteen, and it's rare to see really good muscle definition before seventeen. This doesn't mean that you won't be getting stronger but only that the body hasn't developed a sufficient amount of male hormone to aid in building the bulk that goes along with strength.

It's also important to remember that not all bodies can develop massive muscles. Body type (endomorphic—pudgy; mesomorphic—muscular; ectomorphic—lean) and heredity play vitally important roles in physical development. So when setting goals take into consideration the factor over which you have no control and begin work from that point.

There is also another point to remember. As you've seen in Chapter 6, strength plays a very important role in other sports. Endurance, speed, and flexibility are all functions of strength, and the development of overall strength will make you a better, faster athlete whether you run the hundred-yard dash, swim and dive, or play soccer, baseball, or any other sport.

Here is a workout routine that has been developed expressly for the young body-builder or weight lifter. It's a routine that also will benefit any teenager, boy or girl, whether the desire is to compete in body-building as a sport, to make the varsity in any other sport, or just to get in shape. All of the exercises are adjustable to the individual's strength level.

The workouts here are designed to last about twenty minutes and are to be performed no more than three times a week for at least the first six months. Like all the Mentzer Method exercises, the level of intensity depends on strength. They also can be varied for endurance (light weights/more repetitions) or strength (heavier weights/fewer repetitions).

I think it's important for beginning weight lifters to know where they are when they start by weighing and taking measurements of the arms, chest, waist, neck, thighs, and calves; to keep careful track of the number of workouts, the weights used, and the exercises performed. And do yourself a favor and don't measure your biceps every day or even every week. Real growth takes time, as I've said, and measuring too often is more discouraging than helpful, just as weighing too often can be discouraging to the dieter.

Total body development should be the goal at this beginning stage, so follow all the exercises recommended. If you feel like doing an additional set or two for some body part, go ahead but don't spend a whole workout doing curls because your friend measures a half inch bigger in the biceps. This isn't a race but a steady progression from the rather undefined body of the average teenager to the muscular body of the young adult.

As with all exercise programs, it's important to start with a warm-up. You can use the routine described in Chapter 11 or use the following, which may be a little better suited to the supple teenage body.

EXERCISES FOR TEENAGERS
Front and Back Bend

Stand with your arms extended over your head and your back straight. Touch your knees with your forehead if you can. Return to the starting position and bend backward as far as you can, forming an arc with your back. Repeat 10 times.

Duck Walk

Squat down as far as you can, then duck walk 10 steps forward and 10 backward. Repeat 3 times.

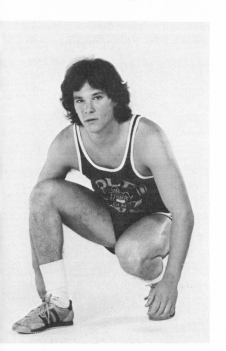

Butterfly Kick

Lie on your stomach with your legs together and your hands at your sides. Raise your chest and legs off the floor and kick as in swimming. Do 5 kicks with each leg, trying to keep your back arched the whole time. Relax in the starting position for a count of 2 and repeat until you've done 20 kicks with each leg.

Side Kick

Roll onto your left side, keeping your legs extended and together. Brace yourself with your right arm and kick the right leg up as far as you can. Repeat 10 times, then roll onto your right side and repeat with the left leg.

Spread Eagle

Sit up and spread your legs as far as you can while keeping your back straight. Reach out with both hands and touch your right foot. Return to the starting position and repeat the move to the left side. Touch each foot 10 times.

Before you go on to the resistance exercises, read the material in this book that explains such matters as breathing, form, sets, reps, overload, soreness, and fatigue.

The Basic Eight exercises in the Mentzer Method are detailed in Chapter 12. They will do just fine for teenagers because they are adjustable to all levels of strength and endurance. That routine and the one in the chapter following it are all you'll ever need unless you decide to dedicate a significant portion of your life to body-building. If you plan to do as I did, then the information and workouts in the chapter on serious body-building will be of interest for the future.

·||| Chapter 16 |||·

EXERCISE IN THE PRIME OF LIFE

I'm continually amazed at the condition of some of the older body-builders I know. Men like Bill Pearl, John Grimek, Ed Corney, and Larry Scott, all over forty, are still in top shape long after athletes their age in other sports have disappeared from the scene. These men still train regularly, maintain their diets, and enjoy a state of mental alertness that allows them to handle two or even three careers at the same time. They all attribute their excellent condition to a lifetime in body-building, a lifetime of intense activity that seemingly has kept age at bay.

But as amazed as I am to see these body-builders, I get an even bigger kick out of some older men and women I see at the gym who have exercised as a hobby rather than as a vocation, and by virtue of making physical activity a part of their life-style, have maintained their bodies, their virility, and their joy of living.

Recently I was riding the exercise bike in the gym when an older man sat down on the bike next to me and started pedaling. I looked over and noticed that he was way up in years, and I thought that maybe he shouldn't be pedaling quite so energetically. I stayed on the bike for a good twenty minutes and when I got off he was still going strong. I couldn't resist asking him how old he was. He said he was eighty-seven. I said, "That's absolutely great! You look like you're in excellent condition and you're still pushing that speedometer up there." "Yes," he replied, "but I used to be able to go a lot faster." I laughed and he did too. I walked away thinking about his wonderful attitude and hoping I would feel the same and look the same at his age.

But he isn't the only senior citizen who is in good shape. We're all so used to seeing pictures of older people who have deteriorated for one reason or another that we forget there are hundreds of thousands of people over sixty who are in great shape and will stay that way until the day they die from natural causes.

I firmly believe that age is more a state of mind than a matter of chronology—if you're healthy, that is. History is filled with examples of people who prove the point:

- Oliver Wendell Holmes served on the Supreme Court in his nineties.

- Clarence DeMar won the Boston Marathon seven times and was still racing at age sixty-nine.

- Francis Bacon did his best work after sixty.

- At eighty, Ellsworth Bunker negotiated the Panama Canal Treaty.

- Gordie Howe played hockey until he was fifty-two.

The list could go on and on, but the point is that despite the many obvious exceptions, society still uses age as a criterion for judging people. But the keys to the quality of life—vitality, stamina, virility—have little to do with age; they depend on physical and mental health.

Since fitness is the key to well-being at any age, what is the current activity level of the "prime time" group? One survey revealed that only 39 percent of people over sixty get any regular exercise, and of that group, almost half cited walking as their favorite form of activity. Of the more vigorous forms of exercise, only 15 percent do calisthenics, swim, bike, run, or train with weights.

Unfortunately, most older people are ill informed about the health, performance, and appearance-enhancing characteristics of exercise, and they have a number of misconceptions as well. Many older people have the attitude that the need for exercise diminishes as they get older; they think the risks of exercise after middle age are too great, they think they don't have the capacity to exercise, and they overrate the benefits of light or occasional exercise. C. Carson Conrad, former director of the President's Council on Physical Fitness and Sports, put changing attitudes at the top of his priority list, saying, "The challenge is one we cannot fail to meet. The stakes are too high. What we are talking about is, quite simply, more years of life and a more abundant way of living for thirty million of our fellow citizens."

Obviously, aging is a process we can't stop, but it's a question of bad news and good news. First, the bad news. Physical, mental, and psychological changes take place as we get older. Physiological maturity is reached in the late teens, and maximum strength and ideal weight in the early twenties. At about twenty-five we reach our physical prime, and this is where athletic ability reaches its peak. But the peak is the peak, and not long after it has been reached, a slow but steady decline begins. Some of the changes include: maximal heart rate decreases, blood pressure increases, aerobic and anaerobic power decline, and respiratory efficiency, strength, and cardiac output go down. Bones become less dense and get more brittle. Joints get weaker, and there is a decrease in endurance and coordination. And inactivity usually causes weight gain, which results in an even lower activity level. This, in turn, causes muscles to atrophy from disuse.

But here's the good news. Fortunately, people differ. A group of ten-year-olds won't really vary much from child to child, but a group of sixty-year-olds can be radically different. Some will be vigorous, trim, and vital; some fat, inactive, and obviously declining; and some will fall in between. What are the reasons for this dramatic variation? Heredity is probably involved, but the main reason is physical activity. The *Physical Fitness Research Digest* says flatly, "The aging process is slowed when the individual exercises as a way of life; and the process is speeded when the individual is sedentary. The values of physical fitness and exercises are not circumscribed by age, they are general and apply in some degree to all ages."

I have the feeling that if a survey were made of people in their fifties and sixties who are still fit, mentally alert, and psychologically intact, you'd find that most of them have been exercising regularly most of their lives. I think you'd also find a surprising number of older, well-conditioned people, especially men, who have used weight training as part of their fitness program.

A number of studies have shown that all the deterioration factors of aging can be slowed with regular exercise, and some of them are actually reversible even in people who have been sedentary for years. Interestingly, the type of exercise doesn't seem to matter much as long as it is vigorous, regular, and frequent. But strength is absolutely vital for vigorous exercise, since strength is necessary to move the body about whether you're walking, running, swimming, climbing, or biking.

So contrary to the mistaken beliefs older people have about exercise, it's good for you at any age. It's never too late to start. There are many research examples. One experimental group consisted of men and women in the seventy-to-seventy-two age range. All trained on an exercise bicycle three times a week for three months. The results showed a decrease in working pulse rate and blood pressure, and an increase in the work load handled and oxygen uptake. There were also positive changes in endurance, agility, coordination, and visual discrimination.

Another study showed that men fifty-five to seventy who had been inactive for a minimum of twenty years improved their aerobic power 20 percent after just eight weeks of training. Similar results were reported in a study of thirty-nine- to sixty-year-olds.

There are some general guidelines for exercise if your age is past forty:

1. The exercise chosen should fit individual exercise tolerance. This means you should be able to do the exercise or series of exercises without undue fatigue. It shouldn't be too easy or too difficult.
2. A higher level of performance can be achieved only by overloading. Increasing intensity or the length of time can both produce overload.
3. Progression is necessary. As tolerance increases with fitness, it's necessary to add to the overload as the body continues to adapt to the increased stress. Progression, or increase in overload, will keep the demands ahead of the body's improvement. Progression can be accomplished by increasing the intensity and duration of the exercise routine.

There are some other things to do as you embark on an exercise program even if you have been reasonably active most of your life. Consider the following points.

MEDICAL EXAMINATION

According to heart specialists, a thorough examination including a stress test is a must if you are over forty even if you've been exercising regularly for a number of years. If you have any heart-related problems, weight training should be very carefully evaluated.

INJURIES

As I've said, muscle and bone weaken with age, and flexibility diminishes as well. In short, you are more susceptible to injury than you were at age twenty. Knees, ankles, hips, and elbows are especially delicate, and ligaments and tendons are more easily pulled, strained, or torn. Even fractures are not uncommon. Considering the possibility of these rather unpleasant and limiting injuries, it's advisable to begin any training program slowly. Test your body, listen to it, and accept its limitations.

PULSE

Check to see what your target pulse rate should be and take your pulse often during heavy exercise. Don't be a hero. Stop working out if you detect an irregular or higher than normal pulse rate for the amount of exercise you are doing.

OTHER SPORTS

There are any number of fitness programs you can pursue, and all of them, performed correctly and with vigor, can produce the kind of results you want. Obviously, I think weight training is the ideal fitness mode, and I recommend that you use the break-in exercises in Chapter 12 for several months before stepping up to more strenuous work. This is true especially if you've been sedentary for an extended period, but I think it's the prudent approach even if you've been active. Weight training is different, it requires the use of different muscles, and it puts a different type of strain on the body. Use your head and listen to your body.

Even a proponent of weight training as a basic conditioner realizes that, if only for variety's sake, it's wise to combine a regular schedule of weight lifting with other exercise, including walking, tennis, swimming, biking, and running.

I'm often asked if any form of exercise is better than no exercise at all. People usually mean bowling, golf, or an occasional stroll in the nearest mall. My answer is an emphatic "no." The primary reason for physical decline is the decrease in the body's ability to transport oxygen— cardiorespiratory fitness. The only way to maintain and improve this ability is through vigorous exercise. Exercise that produces a cardiovascular training effect can slow the body's decline. Regular exercise is the only way to stay young and maintain a high level of fitness and well-being.

·||| Chapter 17 |||·

EXERCISES FOR RUNNERS

The exercises in Chapters 17–20 have been specifically picked to increase strength and flexibility for particular sports. Obviously there is some overlap, since active sports do require the general use of the body's musculature. But specificity of exercise is important. For example, the strength of the wrists and shoulders is vital in tennis and considerably less important in running. Arm and shoulder strength and endurance are crucial in swimming but less important in golf, where the hips, arms, and wrists provide most of the power. The point is, general exercise as outlined earlier provides overall strength development, but further development of the primary muscles used in a given sport is necessary to improve performance significantly—hitting longer off the tee, for example, or improving the velocity of the baseline stroke in tennis.

Specificity of exercise and muscular development is an important point and one that is often overlooked by amateur and professional athletes alike. The only way to improve your skill as a runner is to run. Strength, being a general condition, of course, contributes to the ability to run, but the application of that strength has to be specific to the activity. You can easily prove this to yourself if you're a runner. You may be able to run five or ten miles with relative ease, but when you hop on a bicycle and ride the same distance you'll find that though it seems the same muscles are at work, they really aren't. You'll probably feel considerably more fatigued

149

after riding than you did after running. The reverse is also true. It doesn't help to ride a bicycle long distances in hopes that it will help you run the marathon. It won't. Of course, all exercise is good for the body, but unfortunately, development isn't transferable from one muscle group to the other.

Physiologists feel that the muscles learn to follow movement patterns through repeated practice (neuromuscular training). An exercise that is nearly specific or almost specific won't do the job. The only way to improve your golf swing is to swing the club, eventually achieving that "grooved" swing that is the hallmark of a good player. The swing has to be neuromuscularly trained. Swinging a weighted club may make the club feel lighter when you use it, but in reality it throws your swing and your timing off.

Strength must be built without any consideration of how it will be used. Then the strength can be used in the practice of the sport itself. Using the golf swing as an example, it's possible to develop the gross strength of the wrists and forearms and the hips and apply that strength to the golf swing, leaving the swing itself alone.

These exercises are to be used as adjuncts to the three-day-a-week routine detailed in Chapter 12. They may be performed on off-days or in addition to the regular Mentzer workout, but it's my feeling that the specific exercises should be part of a separate routine and used either once or twice a week. You'll note that the squat and power clean are included for each sport. This is because they are not only good whole-body exercises, but also because they involve the body's major muscle groups, which most of the other movements do not. They also serve as a thorough warm-up for the entire body.

The exercises in this section are primarily for distance runners, since most of us are not sprinters. More Americans are running than are playing racquetball or skiing. The primary reason is for physical fitness, yet to look at most serious runners, you'd think they couldn't move another step. In most cases, the upper body has been eroded while the legs have been strengthened.

These upper-body exercises will increase strength in general and at the same time increase the driving power of the arms; strengthen the back, which will help stabilize the hips and the pelvis, which are critical to good, strong running; and help to balance the muscularity of the frontal thigh and the hamstrings. All of this will serve to strengthen tendons, ligaments, and joints and help to prevent injuries to those high-compression points at the hip, knee, and ankle.

NO. 1: POWER CLEAN AND PRESS

Equipment: Bar and 40 to 50 pounds.

Muscles: Trunk and shoulders, legs and back.

Directions: Stand with your feet about a foot apart and your ankles almost touching the bar. Bend the knees, keeping the head up and the back as flat as possible, and grasp the bar with the hands about shoulder width apart in an overhand grip. Using the strength in your legs, hips, and lower back, bring the bar straight up in a line parallel with the body. When the bar is about chest high, quickly tuck the elbows under and bring the bar to rest on the upper chest, just under the chin. Next, press upward until the arms are fully extended over the head. Lower the bar to the starting position on the floor by reversing the movements. Sets: 2. Reps: 6.

Reminder: Keep the back straight and the head up in the standing position.

NO. 2: PRESS BEHIND NECK

Equipment: Barbell and 20 to 30 pounds.

Muscles: Shoulders and triceps.

Directions: Using a wider-than-shoulder-width, overhand grip, raise the bar to your chest, press it over your head, and lower it behind your head until it rests comfortably on your shoulders. Adjust your hands so that you can get the necessary leverage to press the bar, then press it until your arms are fully extended and your elbows locked. Lower it slowly and carefully to the shoulders. Sets: 2. Reps: 6.

Reminder: Hand spacing is important, so experiment until you find the position that's best for you.

NO. 3: HACK SQUAT

Equipment: Barbell and 20 to 30 pounds.
Muscles: Quadriceps, buttocks, hamstrings, lower back.
Directions: This exercise is performed in the same manner as a regular squat except that the bar is held behind the legs rather than on the shoulders. Begin with the bar on the floor behind you. Bend your knees and pick up the bar with your knuckles forward and then stand up. The bar should be hanging just below your buttocks. With your head up, squat down until your thighs are parallel with the floor or as close as you can come to that position. Pause for a count of 2; then stand up slowly until your legs are straight. Sets: 2. Reps: 6.
Reminder: This is a lower-body exercise, so don't bend your arms when squatting or standing. This exercise puts very little stress on the back, and that's part of its value. If you have trouble keeping your balance, try putting a small board under your heels.

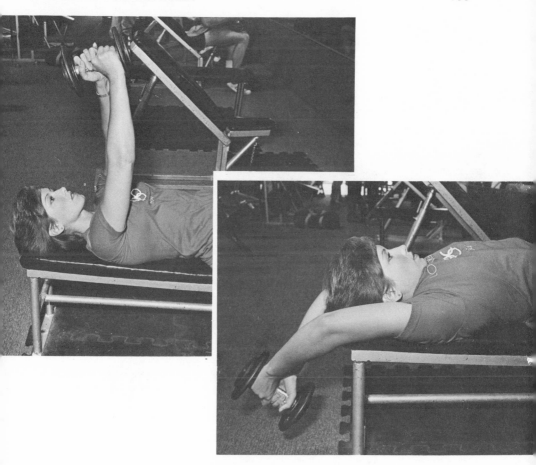

NO. 4: STRAIGHT-ARM PULLOVER

Equipment: Barbell with light weight or a dumbbell.

Muscles: Chest, lats, and stomach.

Directions: Lie on a bench or the floor with the weight directly over your chest, just as in the bench press. Use the overhand grip with the hands a little less than shoulder width apart. Press the weight up until your elbows are locked. Then lower it slowly behind your head as far as you can without any undue pulling. If you're on the floor, lower the weight until it touches the floor. Keep your arms as straight as possible. Slowly bring the weight back in an arc to the starting position. Sets: 2. Reps: 4.

Reminder: Use the muscles in your chest and stomach for this exercise. If you're using a bench, be careful not to go too far back because you can strain your shoulder muscles.

NO. 5: UPRIGHT ROW

Equipment: Barbells and 20 to 30 pounds.

Muscles: Trapezius, shoulders, and biceps.

Directions: Stand with your feet comfortably spread and bend over and pick up the bar with an overhand grip, hands about four inches apart. Stand up, bringing the bar to the arms-extended position at about midthigh. Next, bring the bar straight up along the plane of your body until the bar is just under your chin. Pause at the top for a count of 2 and slowly lower it to the starting position. Sets: 2. Reps: 8.

Reminder: Keep the movement slow and smooth. In the top position your elbows should be a little above your shoulders and pointing out.

These five exercises give the upper body a very complete workout, and the power clean and press and hack squats provide some additional exercise for the legs and lower back. This routine is also a good warm-up for running if you do only one set of each exercise. If you want to do three sets of each at RM weight you should wait several hours before or after running. A third alternative is to substitute the exercises in Chapter 12 and two or three sets of this routine for the day's run. You'll expend about as many calories, and if you move through the sequences quickly, you'll also get the cardiovascular benefit of five eight-minute miles. These exercises will make you a better, more injury-free runner and eliminate pains in the shoulders and neck.

·|||· Chapter 18 ·|||·

EXERCISES FOR THE RACQUET SPORTS

The racquet sports put a premium on anaerobic bursts of energy, quick starts, and quick stops. This puts a strain on the heart but it also puts tremendous pressure on the knees, ankles, joints, and the ligaments and tendons that tie them to the bone. There is also strain in the shoulders, elbows, wrists, and lower back. The following exercises will help to develop these areas, add strength for racquet control and power, and prevent damage to injury-prone areas.

NO. 1: STANDING PRESS (MILITARY PRESS)

Equipment: Barbell and 30 to 40 pounds.
Muscles: Shoulders and upper arms.
Directions: Bring the bar to the chest in the same way you did for the power clean. Spread your feet to provide a firm foundation and then with your head up and back as straight as you can get it, press the bar straight overhead until your arms are fully extended and your elbows locked. Hold it there for a count of 2 and then lower it to your chest. Sets: 2. Reps: 8 .
Reminder: The weight should be kept under control at all times; otherwise balance can be a problem. Do the whole movement slowly and carefully. If you still have a problem, try the press sitting down.

NO. 2: REVERSE CURL

Equipment: Barbell and 20 pounds.

Muscles: Biceps, forearms, and wrists.

Directions: Pick up the bar with an overhand grip and bring it to the midthigh position. Keeping your back straight, your head up, and your elbows in, slowly curl the bar up to your chest and lower the bar under control to the starting position. Sets: 2. Reps: 6 RM.

Reminder: Bring the bar as far up under your chin as you can for maximum results, and keep the movement slow and steady.

NO. 3: DUMBBELL SWING

Equipment: One dumbbell with 10 to 20 pounds.

Muscles: Lower back, quadriceps, and buttocks.

Directions: Spread your legs far enough apart so you can swing the dumbbell between them, and flex your knees slightly. Hold the dumbbell in both hands behind your head as you did for the triceps extension exercise. Then, keeping your arms straight, slowly swing the dumbbell in a wide arc, as if chopping a log, until it passes between your legs. Slowly bring it back to the starting position in the same arc. Sets: 3. Reps: 10.

Reminder: Try to swing the dumbbell as far as you can between the legs or at least until you feel the pull in your hamstrings. Bend your knees as you reach the bottom of the movement, if you need to.

NO. 4: LATERAL RAISE

Equipment: Two dumbbells with 10 pounds on each.

Muscles: Shoulders.

Directions: Stand straight, arms extended at your sides, with a dumbbell in each hand, palms facing in. Raise your arms straight out from the sides until they are at about shoulder height. Slowly lower them back to your sides. Sets: 2. Reps: 6.

Reminder: Keep your feet flat on the floor during this exercise and try not to bounce the dumbbells off your thighs to get them going.

NO. 5: WRIST CURL

Equipment: Barbell and 20 pounds.
Muscles: Forearms.
Directions: Hold the bar in an underhand grip with the hands about a foot apart. Sit on a bench, bend at the waist, and put your forearms on your thighs, with your wrists and hands hanging unsupported. Open your hands and let the bar roll toward your fingertips, bending your fingers down as it rolls. Then use your fingers and hands to roll it back toward the wrist. When you can grasp it again, continue rolling your wrists up and curl the bar up as far as you can. Sets: 2. Reps: 10.
Reminder: Keep the bar under control as it rolls down your fingers or it will end up on the floor.

If you look back over these five exercises, you'll notice that you've worked those areas most important in racquet sports—the shoulders, upper arms, forearms, wrists, lower back, and legs. After six to eight workouts using this routine, you'll notice a definite improvement in your swing and racquet control and you'll probably find that you're getting to the ball more quickly as well. There is certainly no harm in following this sequence three or four days a week, even on the same days you play your favorite game.

·‖‖ Chapter 19 ‖‖·

EXERCISES FOR SWIMMERS

There are actually different resistance exercises for each swimming stroke, but rather than get esoteric, I've selected the five best shoulder, arm, and chest exercises that, combined with the squats and power cleans already described, make a complete workout that will add strength and endurance to your swimming stroke no matter what your specialty.

NO. 1: DIPS

Equipment: Two solidly built chairs with low backs.
Muscles: Shoulders, triceps, and chest.
Directions: Place the backs of two chairs parallel. Put your hands on top of the chair backs in the full extended position with the elbows locked. Then, using only your arms and shoulders for support, lift your feet off the floor and tuck them up as high as you can under you. Next, lower yourself slowly, bending the elbows as far as you can. Then press yourself back up to the starting position. Sets: 2. Reps: 4.
Reminder: This may be difficult at first because you have to balance yourself on the chairs while applying a lot of pressure to raise and lower your body. Practice a couple of times until you get the feel of it.

NO. 2: BACK HYPEREXTENSION

Equipment: A bench.
Muscles: Lower back, buttocks, and hamstrings.

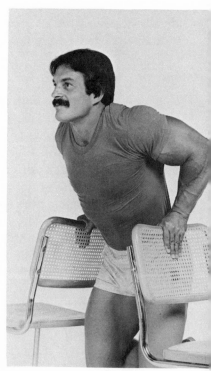

Directions: Unless you have something to hook your heels under, you'll need a partner to hold your legs down for this exercise. Lie face down on the bench so that your body from the waist up is hanging over the edge. With your partner holding your feet, put your hands behind your head and lower your body until you're facing the floor. Then arch your back and raise yourself back to the starting position, arching up past parallel if you can. Sets: 2. Reps: 8.

Reminder: If you have any back problems at all, be careful of this exercise.

NO. 3: BENT-ARM PULLOVER

Equipment: Barbell and about 20 pounds.

Muscles: Chest and shoulders.

Directions: Lie on a bench or the floor with the bar on the floor behind your head. Put your arms over your head and grasp the bar with your palms up and elbows bent. Slowly raise the bar from the floor and bring it over your head into the arms-extended position over the chest. Lower it slowly back to the floor. Sets: 2. Reps: 6.

Reminder: The elbows should be pointing almost straight up when you begin to raise the weight and as you complete the movement.

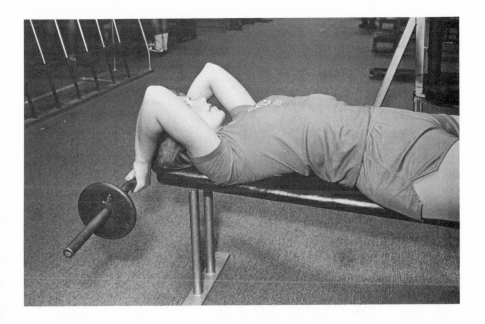

NO. 4: SHRUGS

Equipment: Barbell and 40 to 50 pounds.
Muscles: Trapezius and upper back.
Directions: Using an overhand grip, bring the bar to midthigh with the arms extended fully and the weight resting against your legs. Your feet should be about shoulder width apart. Without moving your arms, shrug your shoulders upward as far as you can. Hold for a count of 2 and then relax. Sets: 2. Reps: 10.
Reminder: This is an upper-body exercise so don't use your arms to raise the weight. All they do is hold the bar and it's moved by the shoulders.

NO. 5: LEG RAISES

Equipment: None.

Muscles: Abdominals.

Directions: Lie on the floor with your legs fully extended and your feet touching with the toes pointing up. Put your hands at your sides or behind your head, whichever is more comfortable. Then, using only your stomach muscles, raise both legs as high as you can without bending the knees. Lower your legs slowly back toward the starting position, but stop when the heels are still a couple of inches off the floor; then repeat. Sets: 3. Reps: 10.

Reminder: Try to bring your legs up until they are perpendicular to the body.

Whether you're a competitive or a recreational swimmer, these exercises will add to your enjoyment. And, of course, this routine can be used as a warm-up before that refreshing dip.

·|||· Chapter 20 |||·

EXERCISES FOR GOLFERS

Golf isn't often thought of as a strength sport, but professional golfers have relatively well-developed biceps, forearms, wrists, and powerful shoulders. It takes strength as well as coordination to boom those drives out, and strength also aids the grip and helps control the club head. Most of the exercises in the section on racquet sports are also good for the golfer, but there are three others that also will add some distance down the fairway.

NO. 1: DUMBBELL CURL

Equipment: Two dumbbells with 20 pounds.
Muscles: Biceps and forearms.
Directions: This exercise can be performed either standing or seated. Take a dumbbell in each hand with an underhand grip and let your arms hang at your sides, palms forward. Either together or alternately, slowly curl the dumbbells up to the chest and then lower them to the starting position. Sets: 3. Reps: 10.
Reminder: Keep the elbows at the sides and try not to move the upper arms at all.

NO. 2: LYING LATERAL RAISE

Equipment: Two dumbbells with 20 pounds.

Muscles: Chest and shoulders.

Directions: Lie on a bench or the floor with the dumbbells at your sides at about shoulder level. Grasp them with palms facing up and lock your elbows. Slowly raise the dumbbells until they meet over your chest. Lower them until they are a couple of inches off the floor and repeat. Sets: 2. Reps: 10.

Reminder: Remember to keep your arms as straight as possible.

NO. 3: TWISTING SIT-UPS

Equipment: None.
Muscles: Stomach and side.
Directions: Lie on the floor with your legs straight and your toes hooked under something solid. Lock your fingers behind your head and curl up as you do for regular bent-knees sit-ups, only this time touch your right elbow to your left knee and slowly lower yourself back to the floor. On the next repetition, touch your left elbow to your right knee. Sets: 3. Reps: 10.
Reminder: The slower you do this exercise the better it is for tightening and strengthening the stomach muscles and the side muscles that help rotate the hips.

There are some specific exercises for other sports as well as these, but I tried to choose the activities that are popular with the greatest number of people. If you're a skier, mountain climber, gymnast, rower, or a team sports player, you can probably figure out your own routine by determining which muscles play the most important role in your sport. Pick two or three of those exercises and add them to the Basic Eight Mentzer exercises and you'll have a specialized program that will meet all your needs.

·||| Chapter 21 |||·

OTHER RESISTANCE EXERCISES

Pumping iron may be the best known and most widely practiced resistance exercise, but there are at least two other fairly popular methods of developing muscular power and strength.

ISOMETRICS

Probably the best known of these is isometrics, a sustained muscular contraction that pits the body's muscles against each other in an internal match-up, either pushing or pulling. The muscular contraction in isometrics occurs with the ends of the muscle fixed in place—there is no joint movement—and significant increases in muscular tension are accomplished without changes in length. If you put the palms of your hands together in front of your chest, elbows out, and press them against each other with all your strength for about six seconds, you'll get a feeling for the contraction isometrics creates.

Isometrics achieved some popularity in this country in the early 1950s when two German scientists, Hettinger and Muller, published their research which indicated that contractions against fixed resistance could increase strength by up to 5 percent a week. (Later research by Hettinger failed to support the 5 percent figure of the initial claim; however, strength increases did occur.)

The beauty of isometrics, and its real appeal to the exercise world, is

174

that the maximum contractions only have to be held for six seconds, once a day, five days a week. Isometrics seem to offer an ideal form of strength development—no equipment is necessary, they can be performed anywhere (even by astronauts in confined spacecraft), they take almost no time at all, and they are injury-free. Yet they do demand considerable outputs of energy and can be fatiguing, and after all, that's what exercise is all about.

They also are useful for certain kinds of rehabilitation and are especially helpful for patients confined to bed. Since no weights have to be handled, a patient in a weakened condition can still exercise and maintain muscle and body tone. Sets of specific exercises have been developed for most of the body's muscle groups.

The basic isometric exercises also can be performed with weights but this method takes more equipment than weight lifting itself, requiring a special "power rack" with a series of stops that limit the movement of the bar and cause an isometric muscle contraction against a fixed object. The combination of barbells and isometrics is called "functional isometrics" and, performed precisely, this method of training can bring the best aspects of both methods into play.

There has been a good deal of research on the validity of isometrics at least partly because the idea is deceptively simple and the results can be surprisingly rewarding. Isometrics also have been compared to isotonic or dynamic exercise in an attempt to determine their relative merits. The results of all this research are not entirely conclusive or consistent, but in general they show:

- Strength gains with isometrics are positive and certain but unpredictable.

- The intensity of muscular contraction in isometrics varies and is difficult to measure.

- With isometrics, strength is developed only at the point in the range of motion where it is applied; this requires several exercises at different angles for each muscle and is imprecise.

- Endurance increases with isometrics but there is no effect on muscular power, flexibility, or the cardiovascular system.

- Isometrics can cut the circulation of the contracting muscles and interfere with the oxygen supply to the muscles; this can produce irregular heartbeats, premature ventricular contractions, and abnormally fast heartbeats.

• Oxygen debt is greater with isometrics, which means it is more anaerobic in nature.

• Recovery from muscular fatigue is slower with isometrics.

• Motivation is lower with isometrics because the results are not easily seen. *

Despite the negatives, however, isometrics offer the serious exerciser a substitute for those times when getting to the gym is impossible, for variety, or in circumstances such as convalescence, when it may be difficult to handle the weights or the machines.

The three major problems with isometrics, however, are the inability to regulate the intensity of exercise, the sometimes negative effect on flexibility, and specificity to the joint angle at which the exercise is performed.

Taking the last point first, isometric training at one point in the range of motion of a joint develops strength significantly at that point but not at other points. Isometric exercises of a gross nature, such as pressing the body up against a bar, do not permit precise applications of contractions to specific muscle groups. This means that each muscle has to be exercised at at least three points in the range of motion, and this necessitates organizing an exercise routine of fifty to sixty different static contractions. This is not only difficult to do, but also, when and if it's finally accomplished, it takes almost as much time to complete as a workout with weights.

The reason that gains in strength from isometrics are not predictable is that the amount of tension applied must be near maximum to be effective. Tests have shown that in reality tension may vary from 25 percent to near 100 percent, but that exercisers were unable to estimate accurately what percentage of total strength they were applying in the exercises.†

---

* *Physical Fitness Research Digest*, President's Council on Physical Fitness and Sports, Washington, D.C., Series 4, No. 1, Jan. 1974.

† Ibid.

Physical Fitness Research Digest sums up its assessment of isometric exercise by saying, "Isometric exercise increases muscular strength; increases muscular endurances, but to a lesser degree than muscular strength; does not affect muscular power; has no known effect on flexibility; does not improve circulatory-respiratory endurance; and may result in trauma if improperly used."

That's not the most positive endorsement an exercise regimen can have, but it doesn't mean that isometrics are all bad, only that they have their limitations. So that you can better judge for yourself, I've included two brief isometric workouts. One uses no special equipment, and one is the functional variety that will require the use of a gym, a power rack, and barbells.

Workout No. 1: No Special Equipment

Curls Sit or stand in front of a table or desk that is too heavy for you to move. Place your hands under the edge with your forearms parallel with the floor. Try to lift the object with a maximum effort and hold for 6 seconds.

Dead Lifts Sit in a chair and place your hands under the seat near your thighs. Contract maximally and try to lift the chair. Hold for 6 seconds.

Shrugs Take the same position you did for the dead lift, only this time try to lift the chair while shrugging your shoulders. Hold for 6 seconds at maximum effort.

Leg Extensions Sit in a chair or on the floor. Flex one leg and grab the ankle with both hands. Try to extend the leg outward with a maximum contraction and hold for 6 seconds. Repeat with the other leg.

Leg Curls Lie on your stomach on the floor or a bench and flex both legs up until you can grab the ankles with your hands. Try to extend the legs against the pull of your hands. Hold for 6 seconds.

Chest Grasp the fingers of one hand with the other and raise your arms to chest level, keeping the elbows up. Try to pull the hands apart. Hold for a count of 6. Reverse the process and try to push your palms firmly together. Hold for 6 seconds.

Workout No. 2: Functional Isometrics

There are only about eight basic movements that can be performed using the power rack, but it's possible to adjust the pins in the rack for an almost infinite number of variations in the same movement. The weight is pulled or pushed until the bar hits the pins and then is held in position for 6 seconds.

The functional isometric exercises—squats, presses, rows, curls— require some muscular retraining because of the limitations imposed by the rack and pins, but the movements can be quickly learned by anyone who has lifted weights on a regular basis.

ISOKINETICS

Isokinetics is a relatively "new" method of strength training that is both isotonic and dynamic and in which the speed of movement is constant against the resistance of a special machine that resists the force applied by the exerciser. Unlike isometrics, however, the resistance allows for movement and results in maximum muscular contraction at a constant speed over a full range of motion.

The special equipment is manufactured by several companies but the most prominent are Cybex and Mini-Gym. Both types contain a control setting that allows a given speed to be predetermined along with the range of motion desired. Some of the equipment has a tension dial that allows the exerciser to see and monitor performance.

The manufacturers claim their devices are the most advanced form of strength building because they develop total specificity, they prevent unstable muscular movements, they are safe and fast.

The benefits of isokinetic exercise have not been researched completely, but the advantage is the mechanically controlled velocity of muscle contraction which imposes maximum resistance. The isokinetic equipment provides constant resistance regardless of the muscular force applied. Training at maximum produces maximum strength gains; the muscles relax momentarily between repetitions and this gives the blood time to clean the lactic acid from the cells that make up the muscle; and all muscles, large and small, are worked in direct proportion to their relative strength.

·‖‖ Chapter 22 ‖‖·

THE TEN MOST COMMON TRAINING MISTAKES

Having trained in gyms all over the world, I've had the opportunity to witness the efforts of literally thousands of weight trainers, and what amazes me is the number of training mistakes I see made by everyone— from the rank beginner to the seasoned veteran. Often these errors are the result of poor concentration or fatigue, but by far the greatest number are the result of sheer ignorance. And while many training mistakes are minor in themselves, their cumulative effect can add up and militate against real progress.

Here are ten of the most common mistakes. They are easy enough to correct but they require some concentration and the awareness that they are, in fact, the kind of problems that can hinder any training effort.

NO. 1: OVERTRAINING

The most pervasive problem among all athletes, not just weight lifters and body-builders, is overtraining. There is a natural and understandable tendency to assume that if a little training is good, then a lot of training is that much better. It is this kind of misdirected thinking that has led serious body-builders to train five or six hours a day, seven days a week.

179

Training too long or too often doesn't allow the body sufficient time to recuperate and replenish the energy resources expended during long workouts. Training every day in any sport uses up the body's reserves that are called up to overcome the exhaustive effects of the exercise. Overtraining also prevents the intense work that is required to stimulate optimal size and strength gains. Remember, you can train hard *or* long but you can't train hard *and* long.

How much training is the right amount for best results? I never train more than four days a week or longer than one hour per session. Sure, sometimes I'll hang around the gym for two or three hours on a workout day, but I make it a point to keep my workouts down to one hour or less. Believe me, I've tried other schedules in the past with the same mistaken impression that more is better. I've learned the hard way that overtraining is probably a more serious mistake than undertraining. Overtraining allows no time for muscle growth or the rejuvenation of the necessary body strength necessary to continue exercising.

NO. 2: LACK OF INTENSITY

Judging from the thousands of questions I receive each year from body-builders and weight lifters all over the world, the nature of size and strength increases is still a mystery to most of them. In fact, it's no mystery at all. For muscles to grow larger and stronger, workouts must be designed to increase stress progressively. That elusive factor is intensity. Less than maximum effort will yield some results but never on the same order as all-out, 100 percent effort. Carrying each set of an exercise to the point of momentary muscular failure, where the completion of one more repetition is impossible despite your greatest efforts, is the only way to force the body to dig into its reserves sufficiently to stimulate an increase in growth.

Anyone with the least bit of training experience knows that progress never comes easily. It must be forced. Adding more sets to your workout isn't the same as training intensely. Increasing the duration of your workouts isn't the same as training intensely. In fact, it will lead to a decrease in the intensity of your efforts because fatigue makes it impossible to continue to perform the movements correctly and with sufficient strength to achieve results.

NO. 3: SLOPPY PERFORMANCE

Barbell exercises that are initiated with a sudden thrust or jerk and continued rapidly to completion actually apply resistance only at the start and finish of the movement. Repetitions that are carried out in a slow and steady manner apply resistance to the entire length of the muscle and are more productive. Once the speed of a movement exceeds a certain rate, momentum takes over and the intensity of muscular contraction is reduced along with results.

In a properly performed exercise the weight should leave the starting position smoothly with no jerking or tugging and proceed on its course in the same manner. If you can't hold the weight in the top, or contracted position, of an exercise without having it fall back to the starting position, then you didn't lift the weight by the force of muscular contraction alone. Your ability to hold the weight in any given position in the range of motion of an exercise is always greater than your ability to raise the weight.

Raising the weight must be accomplished in a steady motion, but lowering the weight has to be done in the same way. Lower it slowly. It shouldn't drop back into the starting position. There is even some current thinking among exercise physiologists that lowering the weight—the negative movement—is more productive than raising the weight. This controlled movement is also a safety factor. Yanking, jerking, or bouncing the weight amplifies the force transmitted to the joints and connective tissues and increases the chance of injury. Lifting heavy weight with proper form using only muscular contraction to do the work rarely, if ever, results in injury.

NO. 4: POOR WARM-UP PRACTICE

It's impossible for muscles to work at an efficient level unless they are warmed up properly. A couple of sets of an exercise, using lighter than normal weights, bring blood and oxygen to the muscle and raise its temperature and contractile abilities. The connective tissues, which are usually cooler than the rest of the body, are thus warmed up, are made more elastic, and are less likely to be pulled or torn. It's not necessary to perform set after set of warm-ups, because two or three sets will do the job.

NO. 5: NEGLECTING MUSCLES

It's extremely important to train all the skeletal muscles without favoring one or two areas you want to develop specifically. You've undoubtedly seen guys with really big arms. The chances are they've neglected other muscles, especially their leg muscles, to achieve that arm development. This results in an unsymmetrical appearance which can become extremely difficult to correct. All the body parts should be trained with the same intensity of effort.

For athletes, neglecting some muscles in favor of others can have serious consequences. The neglected muscles become the weak link in the muscular chain and can result in injury. Football players often train the frontal thighs at the expense of the hamstrings. An explosive contraction of the frontal thigh in a line charge or a sprint out of the backfield can pull or tear the weaker hamstrings.

NO. 6: LIFTING WEIGHTS THAT ARE TOO HEAVY

Egos generally run rampant in gyms of all kinds and especially in weight-training gyms. In an attempt to impress their peers, body-builders and weight lifters try to lift more weight than they can handle properly. At best, in this situation, the lifter fails and walks away with a bruised ego but an undamaged body. At worst, the weight lifter will lose control of the bar and expose himself to a wide variety of injuries.

When lifting heavy weights for training (not ego), it's a good idea to have two spotters close by in case you do fail. Their job is to grab the weight if necessary and prevent an accident that could have serious consequences. The gym isn't a showplace. Never try to lift more than you know you can handle in an ordinary workout. If it's part of your routine to try for maximum single repetitions, be sure to use spotters.

NO. 7: BREATHING

Breathing is an involuntary action and requires no teaching. Maybe because it's so easy, many weight trainers do it incorrectly. They hear it's important to breathe properly when working out so they make it a conscious effort and complicate an otherwise natural function. The most important thing to bear in mind about breathing while working out is to *do* it. Don't hold your breath during heavy exertion. It closes off the glottis in the back of the throat and prevents air from escaping from your thorax. This causes a pressure buildup in the chest and reduces blood flow to the brain. Develop a routine of breathing in which you consistently inhale when raising the weight and exhale when lowering it.

NO. 8: TOO MUCH PROTEIN

Athletes believe that protein is the magic nutritional substance that will make them bigger and stronger and better able to train. While it's true that protein is vital to the maintenance of health and an important factor in cell growth, its role in building strength and improving performance has been grossly exaggerated.

The word "protein" derives from the Greek and means "of first importance," but it does not mean "of only importance." Maintaining health and providing material for growth require over forty different nutrients, most of which can be found in a regular diet of water, carbohydrates, fat, protein, vitamins, and minerals.

NO. 9: ADDING EXCESS BODY WEIGHT

Many body-builders like to add weight to increase strength and build muscle, but you have to be careful because the addition of fat does nothing for strength or appearance. It's impossible for fat to add anything. Increases in muscle mass can come only through high-intensity training, and once growth has been stimulated all that is required is an adequate supply of calories. The body has specific requirements for nutrients, and while it's true that heavy training does increase the need for some of these nutrients, that need is slight. If you can keep in mind that muscle growth is a slow process at best, you may be able to avoid dietary indiscretions that add pounds of shapeless fat.

Beginners who are underweight may experience very rapid weight gains until the body weight normalizes. After that normal weight has been established, however, growth will slow down considerably.

For the body-builder getting ready for competition, the addition of any fat at all will necessitate a restricted diet before a contest to drop the excess. Recent research also indicates that fat buildup within the muscle itself can hinder muscular contraction. This is an obvious disadvantage for any weight lifter. Adding fat is never to your advantage.

NO. 10: POOR ATTITUDE

The first step in building muscular strength is to create a strong image of the kind of body you want. Maxwell Maltz, the developer of psychocybernetics, says, "Psychologists have proved beyond a shadow of a doubt that the human nervous system cannot tell the difference between a real and imagined experience." A strong orienting vision will give your workout the meaning and direction required to develop maximally.

Realistic goals are also important. Dramatic gains are just not possible. Unrealistic goals only set up a pattern of failure that makes it difficult to continue training. If your gains aren't immediate and noticeable, you are going to have to train very hard and consistently for progress. It won't be easy, but nothing that is truly worthwhile is ever easy.

The realization of short- and long-term goals will enhance your self-image and provide the stimuli to continue even harder training. The key to reaching these goals is to be able to summon energies for each and every workout. It's the cumulative effect that results in long-term improvement.

·|||· Chapter 23 ·|||·

CLUBS, GYMS, AND SPAS

As recently as ten years ago a person interested in body-building or weight training had only three choices. Either you trained at home with your own set of barbells, or you went to the "Y," or you went to the local gym. Unfortunately, some of the "Ys" and gyms often resembled medieval torture chambers more suited to the needs of a Torquemada than a ninety-seven-pound would-be strongman. These facilities were all male-oriented. Women had no choices in those prehistoric days.

After one trip to the gym, most people opted for their basement or attic and left the dungeons to the more dedicated. That's one reason why there are so many sets of rusting barbells in closets and garages across the land. Like any other self-improvement program, weight training and body-building have to be pursued with vigor and determination to be effective. Most programs fail in the first month or so because the trainer loses the initial impetus that got him off the starting line, and the motivation of visible progress hasn't appeared.

None of this is to say that you can't do it alone, because I certainly believe you can, but that clubs and gyms do provide a certain amount of camaraderie and motivation not available in your own solitary exercise room. I actually loved the gyms I frequented as a teenager. They were like my own clubhouse. I knew everybody there and they knew me. They were supportive and piled on the praise when they saw progress—and sometimes when they didn't. When I got big enough to start entering contests, the support of the gym gang was invaluable to me. I never minded the dim lights, the noise, or the crowd because they were part of the entire milieu for me, part of a picture that I still look back on fondly.

Things have changed since those recent but relatively ancient days of exercise. Now we have *salons d'exercice,* health clubs, spas of great elegance (and expense), and space-age exercise machinery like the latest in Nautilus equipment, Universal gyms, and the like. Many of these private facilities have equipment that is not only too expensive for private purchase but also too big and bulky for the average apartment or home. Some of the Nautilus clubs have tens of thousands of dollars' worth of equipment and are spread over half an acre.

The types of facilities and equipment are quite varied, offering different things for different people. The variations can be broken down into three basic categories: the traditional gym; the health club or spa; and Nautilus clubs.

TRADITIONAL GYMS

What I call the traditional gym is the kind of second-story space a little off Main Street in most towns, a place where the uninitiated think very strange happenings occur. The "Ys" are also included in the traditional area, and the older "Y" facilities often have the dungeon quality mentioned above.

But these gyms, despite their age and shortcomings, are usually perfectly fine places to exercise and work out. They have all the basic barbell equipment, benches, lat machines, dip and chin bars, mirrors, showers, and most of the necessities, if not the amenities. The big advantages they usually offer are convenience of location and low cost. The average gym or "Y" runs in the neighborhood of $100 to $200 per year, even less in some places, and if you use the facilities on a fairly regular basis, it ends up as a very reasonable investment.

I personally have never been in a gym that didn't contain enough of what I needed for a good workout and usually someone knowledgeable enough to help with the weights if necessary. Very few of these facilities have any kind of formal instruction, however, and that is what most people desire, even those who have been working out for some time.

HEALTH CLUBS AND SPAS

Health clubs are fairly new arrivals on the exercise scene, but in the large cities they have made an impact. Most such clubs are legitimate operations, but an upsetting number are fly-by-night operations whose long-term contracts with members often go unfulfilled, leaving the investor high and dry while the club's organizer wings his or her way to Rio.

The legitimate clubs do offer a fantastic array of fitness-oriented equipment, from exercise bicycles and jogging treadmills to saunas and hot tubs. Many spend a lot of money on pools, fancy offices, and designer clothes for their employees and, therefore, cost a bundle to join. These clubs and spas usually have adequate, if not highly trained, instructors who can keep you from making some of the mistakes in training that can cost you time, but the fancy charts and workout schedules they usually provide are just the extras that allow them to charge the fees they do.

An important thing to keep in mind about the health clubs, especially the larger ones, is that they are not really for the serious weight trainer or body-builder. Nowhere will you find the really heavy weights necessary to develop, nor the atmosphere conducive to serious training. Let out a loud grunt as you try for that last rep and the whole place is likely to turn quiet. You may even get a reprimand from the management. There is a predominantly social atmosphere at most of the clubs and there is certainly nothing wrong with that unless you seriously want to concentrate on building your body.

Costs at health clubs vary greatly, but $300 to $500 a year is more the norm than the extreme. Of course, if you go to one of the live-in spas that have become popular as resorts, the costs increase much faster than the size of your biceps.

NAUTILUS

Some of the latest developments in the world of mechanized weight training have come from Arthur Jones and his DeLand, Florida, laboratory. Jones, an inventor of wide interests, came up with the original design for the Nautilus machines more than thirty years ago, and he has developed his idea into a multi-million-dollar business that has placed his equipment in clubs, private homes, and the training rooms of professional sports teams all over the world.

The Nautilus machines operate with a cam that allows the user to work with weights in comfort and isolate for development muscles that can't be isolated with barbells or dumbbells or some of the Universal equipment now available. A number of well-known body-builders, myself included, work out with Nautilus machines a good part of the time. I find them to be very effective and they somehow make workouts seem a little less arduous. For most people, the novelty of working with Nautilus equipment is enough to get them started and the expense of joining a club is at least some impetus for keeping at it.

One of the things that I've found particularly appealing about Nautilus clubs is the quality of the instruction. The beginner and even the advanced weight trainer can benefit from the training routines and the one-to-one instruction that comes with Nautilus membership. These alone may be enough to recommend the idea.

There is one additional factor that weighs in favor of training in a group setting, and that's motivation. If you have a regular training partner and the two of you are constantly pushing each other to make that heavy rep, it can become an extremely challenging contest. Having a partner also makes it a little harder to skip a workout because, after all, you don't want to look like a lazy lout.

A workout buddy is also a safety device. When working with heavy weights, it's occasionally necessary to get a little aid from your "spotter," who is ever awake to help with the bar if you get in trouble. If you've ever felt you couldn't get the bar off your shoulders after a squat and would have to remain that way until hours later when someone found you in a squashed heap, you can appreciate the value of a spotter.

I suppose I've used every type of equipment yet designed and I've worked out in all kinds of clubs and gyms as well as all those years by myself. I'm as qualified as anybody to recommend one type of facility or another, but I really think it's a matter of personal preference and disposable income. If you can afford it, the clubs are nice and the gyms are fine. If you can't, you can get a perfectly good workout with your own weight set.

·║│ Chapter 24 │║·

WEIGHT AND DIET

Looking back over all my years of training, I'm truly amazed that I made it as far as I did, considering the time I spent pursuing my goals with trusting innocence and complete ignorance. This information gap wasn't quite so pronounced in my training methods, but in the area of diet and nutrition I was totally confused and continually seduced by the magazine advertisements that promised overnight results from this or that product.

I particularly remember one diet supplement that promised a pound a day of muscle gained if you drank a specified amount of an obnoxious powder mixed with milk. In those days I was as enthusiastic as I was ignorant and I bought the whole pitch. In seven months I shot up from 180 pounds to 250 pounds and the only reason I didn't reach my goal of 280 was that the cost of the milk (almost two gallons a day) to mix with the powder was getting prohibitive. I was growing so fast that the stretch marks were getting stretch marks, and I was bursting out of my clothes like Bill Bixby on his way to becoming the "Incredible Hulk."

It took another six months to undo the damage and drop the "bulk" that was then supposed magically to reveal all the new muscle. I actually ended up at a slightly lower weight and with less muscle than when I started.

I suppose I'm a slow learner in some things because this one binge didn't cure me. I continued to read the muscle magazines voraciously, never missing a trick. I knew every fad diet and tried most of them. Of course, I was no different from my colleagues in the continuing search for the particular magic that takes you out of the chorus and makes you a star.

189

All the experimentation, however, did help me realize that almost everything available on the subject of diet and nutrition was pure claptrap, and it spurred me to some serious reading on the subject.

I eventually arrived at a nutritional reality for the body-builder that is applicable to all athletes, and the general public as well. Of course, I didn't invent anything, because a number of nutritional scientists have been telling us for years that the only way to gain (or to lose) weight is to eat more (or less) than we use up. The figure "3,500" is really the magic number. There are 3,500 calories in a pound of fat, which means we have to eat an extra 3,500 calories over basic needs to gain a pound, or cut back 3,500 calories to lose a pound. It's very important, then, to know what our basic needs are. That number is called the Basal Metabolic Rate (BMR). The BMR is a very individual number that represents a person's energy (food) needs to sustain the body in its normal, automatic functions.

The BMR may be individual but there is an easy way to estimate quite accurately the caloric intake necessary to maintain "stable weight." For men: Add a 0 to your weight in pounds (for example, 150 plus 0 equals 1,500) and then add twice your weight in pounds (1,500 plus 150 × 2 or 300 equal 1,800). For women: Add a 0 to your weight in pounds and then add your weight in pounds. The figure you come up with—say, 1,800, as in the example above—is the number of calories your body needs to maintain your current weight. (It doesn't include the energy necessary to meet your activity level, however.)

Going back to 3,500 calories, you can see that it's not all that easy to gain or lose, and you can also see that the extravagant diet claims of losing 1 pound or more of fat a day are simply ridiculous. If your normal intake is only 1,800 calories and you didn't eat anything at all, you'd lose only .5 pound a day, or 3.5 pounds a week. Obviously you have to eat something, so if your normal needs are 1,800 calories and you go on a severe diet of, say, 1,000 calories a day, you'd only lose 1 pound every 4.5 days.

There is another part to the equation, however, and that's your activity level. If you don't change your eating pattern but do begin exercising, you will lose weight because you will be using more calories than you take in. For example, if your BMR is 1,800 and you work out with weights intensely for 30 minutes, you'll use up about 250 calories. That would mean your caloric needs would rise to 2,050 to maintain your weight. If you continued your 1,800 calorie intake you could lose 1 pound in 15 days without dieting at all. That may sound like a long time to lose 1 pound, but in a year it could add up to more than 24 pounds.

So why do people claim that their particular diet works, and why have diet-book writers become very rich? Because diets do work initially for most people. The deprivation of carbohydrates (most starches, sweets, and the good things of life) causes the body to react. Carbohydrates are the body's main source of energy. The low-carbohydrate diet forces the body to reach into itself for other forms of fuel, including some stored fat. This shift in internal chemical processes results in more waste products, and these wastes activate the kidneys. The kidneys respond by getting rid of the waste, and this reduces the body's water content. This loss can conceivably add up to several pounds a week but it's almost all fluid. Since fat is only about 15 percent water, whereas muscle is 70 percent water, the chances are you are losing more muscle than fat.

This immediate weight loss is very gratifying and you may resist the urge for a peanut butter sandwich for a few days or even a week, but by that time the body is sending signals that it wants carbohydrates. You slide back a little and then a little more and pretty soon the diet is forgotten. But if someone asks you if your diet worked, you, of course, give a resounding "yes," having forgotten what really happened.

There is another reason why people go off otherwise successful diets, and that's the problem of "diet plateaus." After a relatively quick weight loss of several pounds at a given caloric level, say 1,500 (down from 1,800), the body begins to adjust to the reduction in fuel. This usually happens in only six or seven days. When the adjustment takes place, your body essentially establishes a new BMR, at around 1,500. This means you have to cut your intake to about 1,200 to continue to lose rapidly. The next reduction would bring you down under 1,000, and that's considered a dangerously low level by doctors and nutritionists.

There has been some experimentation with diets that attempt to outwit the body by going up and down in total calories. For example, cutting to 1,200 for six days and then moving back up to 1,500 for six days and then back down again. There haven't been any conclusive findings on this approach, however. What researchers and the public seem to forget is that the body is very hard to fool. It knows what it wants and needs.

One of the obvious answers to all diet problems is an increased activity level that will help you lose weight (there is some research to show that exercise alone takes off weight) if a sensible diet is followed and maintain that reduction over a lifetime.

Small daily weight gains and losses can usually be attributed to liquid retention or elimination, and this can be deceiving as well. I think it's important to weigh yourself regularly, but I've known some diet fanatics who weigh eight or ten times a day, and their moods—from elation to depression—can hinge on an ounce or two. In most of these extreme cases, the person is a body-builder looking for muscle gain, not just weight gain, as if muscle increased in one-ounce increments several times a day.

And these same people are often in that vast group of innocents deluded by the "pound of muscle a day" claims made by the ads in muscle magazines. It took a long time for it to dawn on me that a pound of muscle a day adds up to 365 pounds of muscle in a year, about ten times more muscle than a person can hope to gain in a lifetime of hard training. And more weight than anyone can carry.

Like dieting, weight lifting can produce almost instant gratification. If you begin underweight and untrained, you can gain several pounds of muscle in a year or so, but once body weight is stabilized at a level near normal for your height, age, and body type, growth will slow considerably despite heavy weight training. A person who begins at or near normal size could conceivably gain 10 pounds of solid muscle after a hard year of training, but even that is a considerable achievement.

Ten pounds a year may not sound like much, but that rate maintained for five years would turn a 165-pound man into a 215-pound knot of muscle. This may not sound outrageous either, but only two of the fifteen competitors at the 1980 Mr. Olympia contest weighed more than 215 pounds.

In theory, too, you would have to eat more to gain weight in muscle. But a pound of muscle is estimated to contain only 600 calories compared to 3,500 for a pound of fat. It is obvious that it takes a lot less food to build a pound of muscle than a pound of fat. This difference is accounted for primarily in the amount of lipids in fat which are high in calories—muscle has 6 percent lipids and fat has 70 percent.

Using the 10 pounds of muscle as an example, that adds up to only 6,000 additional calories in a year—a whole year. That is only 15 or so additional calories a day. A single carrot has more than that. So eating to gain muscle simply makes no sense at all.

BALANCING YOUR DIET

If your BMR plus your activity level is 2,000 calories a day and you aren't gaining or losing weight, then 2,000 is your maintenance level. The chances are, however, that you don't know what you're consuming to reach 2,000. Until you know what you're eating, it's very hard to figure out how to cut down (or increase) consumption, remembering that even a reduction of 100 calories a day will result in the loss of a pound in a little over a month or nearly 12 pounds a year.

Here's an easy way to figure your daily intake. For three days write down everything you eat along with the quantity. Include everything—chewing gum, milk in your coffee, that handful of nuts you almost forgot about. The best way to do it is to carry a little notebook. At the end of the day count up your calories. After three days you'll have a fairly complete picture of your regular diet, and dividing the three-day total by 3 should give you your maintenance level. Don't try to change your diet during the recording days because you won't get the right figure if you do.

It's now possible to plan your balanced diet around your calorie budget with the best combination of macro- and micronutrients, remembering that a surplus of energy (calories) from any source is stored as fat.

Nutritional requirements, including caloric requirements, vary widely among individuals and from time to time in a given individual. Requirements differ with age, sex, body size, psychological state, the level of activity, and the environment where you live.

The conditions that may require adjustments in intake include:

1. Physical activity. Exercise and work increase energy expenditure and food intake (any special needs for nutrients that are related to energy utilization are generally met easily by the increased intake); activity that increases sweating also increases water and salt losses.
2. Heat and cold. Both heat and cold can affect calorie consumption. Cold will result in higher intake, and heat may lower consumption and activity as well. It's not necessary to alter the intake in cold weather, but in prolonged heat it may be necessary, and it is wise to check for the proper intake of essential nutrients.
3. Aging. Body composition changes throughout life, with fat increasing and metabolically active tissues being slowly reduced; there is usually a reduction in physical activity as well; less food will be needed to meet energy requirements.

This simply means that the body generally takes care of its energy needs but that under certain circumstances—especially aging—it may be necessary to make certain adjustments in the diet.

It can't be stressed too strongly that for an individual to maintain proper weight for age, the amount of food consumed over a period of time must *closely* reflect energy needs.

Many nutrients can be tolerated well in amounts that exceed the recommended allowances by two or even three times, but energy intake (calories) in excess of requirements is highly undesirable and can lead to obesity.

The 1980 National Academy of Science publication *Recommended Dietary Allowances* says: "It cannot be emphasized too strongly that, although there are some who ardently encourage the ingestion of excessive amounts of several individual nutrients, the Committee is *not* aware of convincing evidence of unique nutritional benefits accruing from the consumption of a large excess of any one nutrient or combination of nutrients." This includes the highly controversial use of vitamin C recommended by Dr. Linus Pauling.

The healthy body needs energy for the metabolic processes to support physical activity, for growth, and to maintain body temperature. There are those people who seem to eat the amount of energy appropriate to their age, sex, and weight but still add excessive body fat. The way to remove this problem is not necessarily dieting but increasing the level of physical activity until the desired weight is reached. There are reasons for this:

1. Appropriate energy consumption is necessary for the efficient use of protein for growth and maintenance.
2. It is difficult to ensure the nutritional adequacy of diets that are lower than 1,800 to 2,000 calories in energy content.
3. Evidence indicates that a sedentary life-style contributes to degenerative arterial disease, obesity, possibly diabetes, and other complications. One body of research has indicated that daily consumption of an excess of only 84 calories per day will add nearly 10 pounds of fat in only a year.

Ideal weight or average weight is highly individualized and difficult to establish for any group in the population. But according to the National Center for Health Statistics, the average American male adult is 5 feet, 10 inches and weighs 154 pounds, and the average female is 5 feet, 4 inches and weighs 120 pounds. But body composition changes throughout adult life because of a natural loss of lean body mass, which is then replaced by fat. This results in a lowering of the BMR by about 2 percent per decade after age 21.

Activity is the dominant factor in the variability in individual energy needs—that is, the proportion of time people spend in moderate-to-heavy activity as opposed to light or sedentary activity.

Since some people work hard physically and then relax, and other people work in a sedentary job but play hard, it makes no sense to try to express energy needs by job categories or occupations. But the government has established the adult energy requirement for health maintenance with moderate activity at about 1.7 times the BMR for men and 1.6 times the BMR for women. This figure may be adjusted slightly upward for people with larger bodies or who weigh more but are within shouting distance of their ideal weight. One problem is that a person who is really overweight often compensates for the higher energy cost of carrying that weight by decreasing the daily activity level.

MACRO- AND MICRONUTRIENTS, CARBOHYDRATES, AND FIBER

Energy to run the body can come from any reasonable combination of carbohydrates, fat, and protein, and even alcohol contributes energy to some extent.

Briefly, the principal carbohydrates are sugars, starches, and cellulose, or fiber. The sugars include the monosaccharides and disaccharides in refined sugars, jams, jellies, syrups, honey, fruits, soft drinks, and milk. The starches are the polysaccharides of cereals, flour, potatoes, and other vegetables.

There has been recent excitement over the importance of dietary fiber (indigestible carbohydrates that provide bulk in the diet and aid in elimination) among some nutritionists and health buffs. According to the most recent studies (Reilly and Kirsner, 1975; Spiller and Amen, 1976; Roth and Mehlman, 1978), the hypothesis that increased fiber intake will help reduce cardiovascular disease, colonic cancer, or diabetes is plausible but has not been proven experimentally.

Although its physiological significance hasn't been adequately explored, the federal government says, "For the general population, moderate increases in dietary fiber consumption achievable by increased consumption of vegetables, fruits, and whole-grain cereal products are desirable."

Man, like most mammals, is capable of converting amino acids and parts of fats into glucose, and as a result there is no specific dietary requirement for carbohydrates, although 50 to 100 grams per day is a reasonable amount. On the other hand, it's interesting that a diet without carbohydrates (the approach of many popular diet programs) can lead to excessive breakdown of tissue protein, loss of sodium, and involuntary dehydration. High-fat diets and fasting can cause these conditions as well. Fruits, vegetables, and whole-grain cereals provide energy principally from carbohydrates and are also good sources of vitamins and minerals.

FAT

The body's cells can use fat as a direct source of energy. Carbohydrates are the preferred source of energy, but a period of starvation (such as dieting) can force the utilization of fatty acids and amino acids. Most of the fat in foods occurs as triglycerides that are fairly tasteless, but in combination with other nutrients they provide palatability and they contribute to a feeling of fullness. Most fat foods, either animal or vegetable, are easily digested.

Fats are necessary without question, but an excess of energy in the body, whatever the source, is stored as fat, which helps insulate the body and cushion the organs, but excess fat stores result in overweight and its attendant problems.

There is no specific requirement for fat as a nutrient in the diet, but 15 to 20 grams per day is appropriate according to the federal government.

PROTEIN

The body has natural proteins, and food proteins provide amino acids (there are nine essential amino acids) for the synthesis of these natural proteins. Protein consumed in excess of the amounts needed is rapidly degraded and removed by the body, primarily in the urine. It has been rather firmly established that an intake of .75 gram per kilo per day contains a safety margin and is actually more than enough for maintenance and growth. To figure your own needs, multiply your weight in kilograms (1 kilo equals 2.2 pounds) by .75 or figure that you need less than 1 gram of protein for every kilo of body weight.

There is little evidence that muscular activity increases the need for protein, and in view of the margin for safety in the recommended daily allowances, no increase is needed for work or exercise. And, according to the federal government, "There is no compelling evidence to show that higher intakes of protein are either beneficial or harmful."

SUMMARY OF GOVERNMENT RECOMMENDATIONS

Based on a diet of 2,000 calories per day, the total fat intake should not exceed 35 percent of daily caloric consumption, or about 700 calories. Carbohydrates, long considered the culprits in any kind of diet, should constitute 50 percent or 1,000 calories a day because carbohydrates not only help provide necessary vitamins and minerals but also are important for proper intestinal function. And protein intake should be only about 15 percent or 300 calories in the daily diet.

The macronutrients—carbohydrates, fat, and protein—are only part of the nutritional story. The micronutrients—vitamins and minerals—are also vital to the functioning of a healthy body.

VITAMINS

Vitamins are organic substances that play a major role in the control of the body's metabolic processes. The body cannot manufacture its own vitamins, so they must be obtained from the daily diet. Daily requirements are very small and if you are eating a well-balanced diet, then you are certainly getting all the vitamins you need naturally.

Nutritionists seem to agree that vitamins are essential to good health, but there is no agreement on which vitamins (if any) are most important or who needs them. It is clear, however, that vitamins, even in massive doses, do not cure disease or provide extra health protection, and this includes vitamins C and E. In fact, the government reports "a number of adverse effects of excessive intakes of ascorbic acid" (vitamin C), and that "routine consumption of large amounts of ascorbic acid is not recommended without medical advice."

Ronald Deutsch, one of the country's most outspoken nutritionists, says, "In extra doses, used essentially as medicines, vitamins and minerals cure scarcely anything except deficiencies in vitamins and minerals."

One other point is important. Vitamins do not provide energy, and there is absolutely no need to increase your vitamin intake even during heavy exercise if you are eating a proper diet.

MINERALS

Minerals are chemicals found in the soil and passed to humans through plants and animals. Minerals are vital to life processes but only in small quantities. Minerals most needed by the body are sodium, magnesium, calcium, and potassium. Most minerals can be obtained from a daily diet that includes vegetables, fruits, grains, and dairy products.

WELL-BALANCED DIET

The well-balanced diet for the average person is qualitatively the same as the diet for the athlete. Nutritionists have divided foods into four groups based on similarities in nutritive value and their relative role in the diet. The following are recommended:

• Meat group—two or more servings per day of meat, fish, poultry or eggs with serving size averaging about three ounces

• Vegetables and fruits—four or more servings per day

- Dairy group—two or more servings per day of milk, cheese, butter, or ice cream

- Breads and cereals—four or more servings

The basic four will provide all the micro- and macronutrients needed by the average person, and there should be no need for vitamin or mineral supplements of any kind.

This does not mean that there aren't times when supplements are useful, only that in this country those times are rare unless your diet is completely unbalanced. Consultation with your doctor is wise if you think you have a vitamin or mineral deficiency.

WEIGHT LIFTING FOR THE SERIOUS BODY-BUILDER

·||| Chapter 25 |||·

THE PHYSIOLOGY OF MUSCLE GROWTH

The facts are basically simple. Human beings are designed to move. The brain is the source of the signal to the central nervous system that in turn causes movement. The evidence—the only evidence—of these brain signals is seen in muscular movement.

There are three kinds of muscles in human beings: the smooth muscles on the inside of the body, the heart muscle, and the skeletal muscles. Each muscle is a bundle of fibers (the number of which is determined before birth) that join into a tendon at each end. The bundles are activated by a motor nerve that originates in the central nervous system. Muscles all serve a specific function and are confined to a given space.

The skeletal muscles are elongated and cylindrical in shape and their thickness varies between or among muscles and even within the same muscle. All stimuli affect the muscles—skeletal, smooth, and heart—activating them and causing them to shorten. Strength depends on the size of the muscle, and strength can be developed only through progressive resistance exercise.

These are the facts, but somehow they have eluded most body-builders. Within the rather tight-knit world of body-building, the training practices of the top champions, not physiological truths, have assumed the status of commandments. Many of these beliefs regarding training and the building of muscle tissue had their origin decades ago with title winners like Reg Park and Steve Reeves. And they have lived on. Most of these accepted beliefs are without scientific basis, yet they have become dogma and continue to misguide aspiring body-builders. Since there is no logical consistency to this conventional wisdom, body-builders, regardless of age or experience, often pursue their training in confusion and uncertainty.

The traditionalists would have us believe, for example, that because we are individuals and unique, the facts presented above don't apply and, therefore, each of us must need a different training program to make our muscles grow. While it is true that we all respond to training at varying rates (due to variations in age, physical condition, and innate adaptability), the requirements for muscle growth are universal and apply with very little variation to us all.

This confusion is primarily responsible for the high dropout rate among serious body-builders. The uncertainty surrounding training causes continuous, almost hysterical changing of routines in the hopes of eventually hitting on something that will yield the desired results.

These poor souls should realize that there is no mystery involved in muscle growth. The cause-and-effect relationships have been known and studied for decades. The biochemical changes that result in muscle growth for Mike Mentzer are essentially the same for everyone. If this was not so, medicine would not be a science but a series of studies of individual physiologies.

The logical conclusion follows the facts. The stimulus required to induce those biochemical changes that result in muscle growth is also universal. The stimulus is physical exercise that produces progressive alterations in the body's various capacities, including muscle size and strength.

The body's adaptive mechanism is versatile and can respond to many forms of stimulation, and while any form of stress can, and will, elicit an adaptive response, the form of adaptation always will be specific. If you are seeking a specific adaptive response, such as increased muscle size or endurance, then a specific form of stress must be imposed. The fact that specific demands result in specific physiological adjustments to those demands has been known for a long time and is referred to by exercise physiologists as "specificity."

I've talked about intensity and duration. Intensity was the one specific element of exercise required for stimulating increases in muscular size and strength. It is the duration of exercise that was the key to endurance. The intensity factor, then, is the most important to body-builders and strength athletes. Intensity of effort is important, but it must be high enough to induce an adaptive response. As a rule of thumb, the intensity factor must exceed 50 percent of one's existing capacity. The more the intensity exceeds 50 percent, the greater the rate of improvement. Those interested in inducing maximum muscle size and strength must exercise regularly at or near the 100 percent intensity level.

Among the reasons for lack of success of many body-builders is the failure to understand specificity. This lack of understanding has led to training that results in improvement in their endurance more than muscle building. Those who train according to convention train too often, usually every day, and too long, two to four hours per session, to stimulate much in the way of muscle size. Training too often and too long prevents high-intensity training and, therefore, limits progress as well as size and strength gains.

Most serious body-builders desire to build as much pure muscle as possible, as opposed to developing total fitness. If this is the case, then lowering the intensity to any level below 100 percent will compromise that goal. Intensity of effort is the most important factor in stimulating size and strength increases in skeletal muscle tissue. Only high-intensity muscular contraction can stimulate the growth mechanism in the muscle itself.

Thus carrying a given exercise or set to the point where it's necessary to use 100 percent of the momentary muscular strength is the single most important factor in increasing size and strength. Working to this "point of muscular failure," where another rep is impossible, ensures maximum growth. Obviously, this forces a reduction in the amount of time you can spend training.

·||| Chapter 26 ||·

ADVANCED BODY-BUILDING

The vast majority of people who take up weight training and body-building do so for noncompetitive reasons. They are pumping iron for fitness, appearance, or both. Others, however, take up the sport with the idea of becoming competitive. They think they can do it and they want to give it a try.

If you're interested in competition, you can begin at almost any level of development. My own competitive career began at the age of eighteen in Lancaster, Pennsylvania, near my hometown of Ephrata. The local YMCA sponsored a Mr. Lancaster contest under the auspices of the AAU, and I won. These small, local competitions are important for providing motivation for aspiring young body-builders, and winning my first contest certainly spurred me on. I entered a statewide meet, won that as well, and became Mr. Pennsylvania.

At nineteen I decided to take another step and entered the 1971 Teen Mr. America contest. I placed second. Some months later I took a credible tenth place in the prestigious Mr. America meet. (At present there are few restrictions for entrants in physique competitions. Any body-builder with reasonable development can enter.)

After years of playing team sports I decided I needed an arena where I alone could excel. Physique competition, among the most individual of sports, filled that need.

The training in the gym is an isolated activity, and the effort required comes solely from the individual with only occasional help from training companions. And even more singular is the competition itself. In the darkened auditorium, standing center stage, spotlighted from above, I stand alone displaying the fruits of my labor, and to me personally belongs either victory or defeat.

Throughout my competitive career I've always felt it is the effort, the actual challenge of attaining a peak of condition, that is most rewarding. Winning or losing ceases to be the prime concern. The privations imposed by strict dieting, along with the discipline required to improve my physique further through very intense training, impart a sense of meaning and fulfillment to my everyday life. The strength of character that comes as a direct result of such training and competition has served many of the top champions, who have retired from competition and moved on to become successful doctors, lawyers, actors, or businessmen.

The primary motivation of the body-builder is, as the name implies, to build his or her body by developing larger-than-average muscle mass uniformly over the entire body. Judging from my own experience and from listening to countless others, it has become obvious that the desire for added mass is always a strong motivation, whether the individual is a rank beginner or a Mr. Olympia.

The moment a body-builder considers entering a competition, however, the acquisition of more muscle mass ceases to be the primary motivation. The criteria by which physiques are judged have been codified by the Amateur Athletic Union (AAU) and International Federation of Body-building (IFBB). They include, in addition to overall muscular mass or size, muscular definition (very low body fat), symmetry, overall appearance, and posing and presentation. Each of these things plays an equal role in the judging of a physique contest, and the serious competitor must divide his work and attention equally among these once he begins his contest preparation. Preparing for a contest is an art in itself and takes years of experience to master. Over my years of competition I have kept a journal with accurate records of my various contest preparations. And while the individual can gain the confidence and stage presence that are important assets in competition through experience only, there is much he or she can learn from the experience of others.

ASSESSING YOUR CONDITION

If you are seriously thinking of entering competition, check with the local or regional AAU chairman for dates of events, or check the schedules printed in the muscle magazines. You must allow yourself enough time to make the required modifications in your training and diet which will enable you to reach a peak of condition on the day of the contest. You are in peak condition when your body composition is such that you've maintained all the muscular mass you've accumulated and have eliminated all traces of body fat. The amount of time needed to prepare will hinge largely on the body-fat level. The leaner you are, the less time will be required. The primary goal is to get as much definition as possible while at least maintaining your existing muscle mass. During preparation the development of size is not the only concern, as it is difficult for the average trainer to build muscle and lose fat simultaneously. It is not impossible but it requires too much attention to certain details, time that is better spent in other ways.

A person can use several methods to assess how much of his body weight is composed of fat. The most expensive and sophisticated but least practical for the average body-builder is a radioisotope assay test. Less expensive and much more accessible are hydrostatic weighing and skin-pinch calipers.

Hydrostatic (underwater) weighing involves being weighed first in the regular manner and then underwater. Since muscle is denser than water, the person's lean body mass will sink and be weighed while fat, which is less dense, will float and not be counted. This is why lean people sink in water more readily than fat people do.

By using certain standard calculations, the difference between dry weight and water weight will tell how much body weight is fat and how much is muscle or lean mass. This can be very helpful, especially for beginning competitors. By knowing exactly how many pounds of fat are on the body, you can calculate how much time will be required to reach a level where the percentage of body fat is consistent with that condition body-builders call "ripped," usually 3 to 6 percent of overall body weight.

Information on how to calculate and time fat losses can be found at facilities with hydrostatic weighing tanks, through exercise physiology labs on college campuses, or at commercial establishments that perform physiological tests.

The skin-pinch caliper test is much simpler and involves the measurement of skin thickness over the muscle on various parts of the body, usually the biceps, triceps, latissimus, and lower back area. These measurements can then be compared with a standard chart, and the assessment of body-fat levels can be made. The calipers range in price from $7 to $150, and can be found in medical supply stores.

All the techniques have a margin of error that is difficult to account for. The simplest and least expensive method for assessing the body is to look in a mirror. Are your chest muscles, the pectorals or "pecs," clearly delineated around the edges, giving them a squared-off look? Can you grab fat in the nipple area, or is the skin tight and close to the muscle? What about the area around your navel? Does it jiggle, or is it tight with no visible roll of fat? Another area where fat tends to accumulate and provides a good indication of your overall condition is the lower back on either side of the spine right above the hips. If you can grab an inch or more of fat in that area, you will probably need up to ten weeks of rigid training and dieting to get ripped.

At any rate, six weeks should be the minimum time allocated to prepare for competition, and anything more than ten weeks becomes too taxing and draining. If you tend to be lean and need to lose only eight to twelve pounds, spend a solid six weeks training and dieting. If you think you need to lose more than twelve pounds, then take eight to ten weeks. Figure it this way: Even on the most severe diet, the maximum body fat you can possibly lose in one week is about three pounds. At that rate you could lose eighteen pounds in six weeks, allowing no time for error or backsliding. Actually it's best to reach a peak one or two weeks before a contest and hold it rather than to train and diet until the last minute. The last week should be spent practicing your posing and relaxing so that you'll be strong and refreshed on the day of the contest.

TRAINING

Remember that you have embarked on a course of contest preparation, and acquiring additional size is not terribly important. Your training should be aimed at maintaining existing mass while you lose as much body fat as possible. The maintenance of muscle is relatively simple if you stick to regular workouts like the typical four-day-a-week split routine and employ the pre-exhaustion techniques mentioned in Chapter 27. Mass can be maintained. Severe workouts involving ultraheavy weights that allow only three to five reps aren't necessary, but can't hurt if performed occasionally. Since you'll most likely be on a reduced-calorie diet while preparing for competition, you'll find intense workouts very draining.

Advanced training methods like forced reps, negatives, or rest-pause should be done infrequently—once a week at most—and only after a two-day layoff. This all depends on the individual's energy level and training plan. As a rule of thumb, however, carry each exercise to a point where you can't lift the weight any more—a point I call "positive failure." And again, include forced reps, negatives, and rest-pause training only periodically when you have an abundance of energy and strength. Under no circumstances is a six-day-a-week training schedule advisable.

STEROIDS

Scientific and technological discoveries have entered every area of modern life, and advances in nutrition and physical conditioning have had a startling impact on modern athletics as well. A glance at the records of recent Olympic games shows the true impact of the application of some of this knowledge. In many events, the records held by today's women far exceed the records set by men in the 1936 Olympic games. Compare the top physique stars of twenty years ago to today's titleholders and the picture is even more graphic. That past Mr. America wouldn't even place in today's contests.

The reason isn't the kind of straight physiology, intensity, and duration of training I've been talking about. Body-builders, like so many other athletes, have made use of the recent developments in chemistry. Because of the overemphasis on drugs like the steroids—a magic potion so seductive that many body-builders ignore training and nutrition in favor of the little pills—I've been reluctant to pursue the subject publicly. But I've finally become convinced that because young body-builders and other young athletes are easily tempted to take body-building drugs, it's important for them to be informed of their effects.

The oral anabolic steroids, especially Dinabol, are the most widely used of all the body-building drugs. They are a refinement in this particular class of drugs whose properties have been known since the 1770s, when Dr. John Hunter transplanted the testes from a rooster to a hen and induced male characteristics. In 1849 Berthold transplanted testes into castrated roosters and thus prevented signs of castration. This testicular principle was further defined by Laqueur in 1935 and named "testosterone."

These testosteronelike synthetic drugs have anabolic (tissue-building) and androgenic (development of male secondary sex characteristics) properties. It is the anabolic action that is important in athletic performance. Anabolics assist in nitrogen retention, prevent the body's protein—its building blocks—from being broken down into glucose and fat, and help incorporate protein into the muscles.

The desired effect for athletes, particularly body-builders, wrestlers, weight lifters, and football players, is an increase in muscle bulk, weight, and strength, and improved performance. It isn't clear, however, if this actually is what happens.

A report from the American College of Sports Medicine found that anabolic steroids do not of themselves "bring about any significant improvements in strength, aerobic endurance, lean body mass, or body weight." But more importantly, the report states, "There is no conclusive scientific evidence that extremely large doses of anabolic-androgenic steroids either aid or hinder athletic performance."

This should be eye-opening for the athlete who takes up to 500 milligrams a day in the hopes of improving performance, especially since the potential side effects of steroids can be very serious. The drugs almost certainly cause liver damage in men and women, and can result in decreased natural steroid output from the testes, pituitary dysfunction, and sexual impotency. In women the undesirable side effects can include masculinization, voice change, acne, growth of facial hair, and menstrual irregularities. If steroid use is continued over a long period the effects can be even more severe for women—baldness, excessive body hair, prominent veins, and enlargement of the clitoris. Very long-range effects are still unknown.

I think the real decision rests with the individual after all the facts have been studied. If the athlete thinks the real (or possibly placebo) benefits of taking the anabolic steroids outweigh the potential risks, so be it. I doubt, however, that many people will accept a life of liver impairment, and a generally uncertain health prognosis in exchange for the adulation of the crowd, a trophy, and a handshake.

Chapter 27

MIKE MENTZER'S WORKOUT

If you've been training at least a year and have made good progress in developing muscle size and strength, you may have the potential to go on to bigger things. By now your body has grown accustomed to the demands of weight training and you no longer look toward workouts with apprehension and a sense of impending discomfort. In fact, it's probably just the opposite. You feel physical discomfort when you're forced to miss a workout because your muscles have come to thrive on heavy efforts. The weights have become a positive addiction.

As I've said before, almost any type of training program will result in temporary progress. This is because the departure from no training to activity places some overload on the body and will stimulate the body's adaptive mechanism to compensate through size and strength increases. This progress is naturally limited and a plateau is soon reached. This plateau will be left behind when the body is called on to perform more demanding exercise.

This intermediate step up involves more complicated training principles and considerably higher intensity levels. Because the workouts are more demanding, I suggest using the split routine—dividing the body parts and working only half the body each session. Full-body workouts can still be used but you may find they leave you too exhausted to carry on the activities that comprise the rest of your daily life.

The increased intensity will be provided by using forced repetitions, negative resistance, pre-exhaustion exercises, and a reduction in training time.

FORCED REPETITIONS

Remember that intensity is defined as the percentage of momentary effort a person is capable of generating. Regular attempts to perform the momentarily impossible must be made, since repeating tasks already within your capabilities will do little to stimulate growth. Forced repetitions will literally "force" you to work beyond your established limits.

In performing forced reps, choose a weight for each of the exercises that allows for approximately eight reps in good style. When you've completed eight or as many reps as possible, have your training partner help you complete two additional "forced" reps. This help should be just enough for you barely to finish the two reps using your greatest efforts. The idea is to raise the intensity by exerting the last bit of your momentary ability.

NEGATIVE RESISTANCE

Skeletal muscles have three levels of strength: concentric—the ability to raise the weight; static—the ability to hold the weight; and negative, or eccentric—the ability to lower the weight. Our ability to raise or lift weights is the weakest. The ability to holds weights for a given length of time at any point in the range of motion of an exercise is greater than the ability to raise the weight. The ability to lower is the greatest of the three. The ability to lower the weight after performing eight strict reps and two forced reps is still available, and unless you exhaust the remainder of your abilities, you haven't trained to the point of total muscular failure.

After completing the last forced rep of a set, continue with negative reps by having your partner lift the weight to the concentric position so you can continue lowering it. The first two or three negatives should be easy and you should be able to lower the weight slowly. You'll even be able to halt the downward motion of the weight during these first few negatives, since your static level of strength is still intact. As you proceed with the next two or three reps, the downward speed will increase and you'll lose control of the weight. By this time your static strength will be exhausted, although you should have enough negative strength available to perform two more reps.

Terminate the set when you can no longer control the downward motion of the weight. It's not wise to perform negatives at the end of every exercise, each and every workout. Negatives enhance the intensity of your workouts dramatically but increase the possibility of overtraining. Do negatives once a week for each body part. It's not necessary to do them for all body parts in the same workout.

PRE-EXHAUSTION EXERCISES

It's only logical that if intensity of muscular contraction is the single most important factor affecting size and strength increases, the largest and most rapid increases can result only when our effort is 100 percent. With conventional barbell and dumbbell exercises, it's not always possible for the muscles to exert 100 percent of their contractile ability because of "weak links."

Power exercises—bench or incline presses—aimed primarily at working the pectoral muscles involve the smaller and weaker triceps on the back of the arm. A point of failure of an exercise like the incline press is reached when the weaker triceps fail. This is well in advance of the bigger and stronger pectorals, thereby preventing the pecs from ever reaching failure and receiving the fullest possible growth stimulation.

The same situation exists when working the latissimus muscles with conventional exercises like barbell rows, chin-ups, or pulldowns on the lat machine. The smaller and weaker biceps are unavoidably involved with the bending of the arm in these exercises, and here again, a point of failure will be reached when the biceps give out in advance of the latissimus muscles. This will leave them largely unstimulated.

Such weak links can be overcome by performing an isolation exercise immediately prior to a compound exercise. An isolation exercise works primary muscles such as the pecs and allows them to contract without involving auxiliary muscle groups such as the triceps or biceps. A compound exercise does not involve an auxiliary muscle while working a primary one. Performing an isolation exercise—dumbbell flys, cable crossovers, or Nautilus flys—to the point of momentary muscular failure will pre-exhaust the pecs while preserving the strength of the triceps. Following the isolation exercise immediately ("zero rest") by a compound exercise—dips or incline presses—will enable the fresh triceps to serve the pecs, which are now exhausted. The temporary strength advantage of the triceps will cause the pecs to continue working close to 100 percent of their momentary ability. The delay between the isolation and compound exercise must literally be zero because even a three-second delay will allow the primary muscles—pecs, in this case—to recover up to 50 percent of their strength and make the auxiliary muscles, the triceps, weak links again. After the isolation-compound cycle has been completed, there can be a short rest period.

REDUCING TRAINING DURATION

Intensity involves performing the same or more work in less time, in addition to handling heavier weights. Because high-intensity training is so demanding, don't attempt to hurry through the workout at first. As you adapt to the increased stress, gradually reduce the duration of your workout. It may take up to an hour and a half to complete the suggested routine at first, but in time it can be reduced to a little more than thirty minutes.

THE WORKOUT

Monday and Thursday

Legs:	1. Leg extensions	1 cycle
	2. Leg presses	
	3. Squats	1 set
	4. Leg curls	1 set
	5. Toe raises	2 to 3 sets

Alternate isolation exercise: The leg extension is the only exercise that effectively isolates the frontal thighs. If a leg-curl machine is not available, hyperextensions or stiff-legged dead lifts will substitute.

Alternate compound exercises: If you don't have a leg-press machine, perform squats immediately after the leg extensions and do cycles.

NOTE: As the squats involve the use of much heavier weights and can be dangerous to the lower back if proper caution isn't exercised, I suggest that you choose a weight that allows approximately ten reps and stop at the point of positive failure rather than go on to total failure with negative reps.

| **Chest:** | 1. Dumbbell flys | 2 cycles |
| | 2. Incline presses with barbell or dumbbells | |

Alternate isolation exercises: Cable crossovers, a pec deck, or the Nautilus chest can be used in place of the dumbbell flys.

Alternate compound exercises: The bench press, dips, or decline press can substitute for the incline presses.

Triceps:	1. Triceps pressdown	
	2. Dips	2 cycles

Alternate isolation exercises: French presses, cable extensions, Nautilus triceps extensions, and barbell extensions are isolation exercises.
Alternate compound exercises: Close-grip barbell bench presses or bench dips.

Tuesday and Friday

Lats:	1. Stiff-arm pulldown on lat machine	
	2. Close-grip, palms-up pulldown	2 cycles
	3. One-arm dumbbell row	2 sets

Alternate isolation exercises: Nautilus pullover, and pullovers across bench with either barbell or dumbbells.
Alternate compound exercises: Barbell rows, cable rows, and close-grip, palms-up chins.

Traps:	1. Shrugs	
	2. Upright rows	2 cycles

Alternate isolation exercises: Shrugs can be done with a barbell, dumbbells, or on the Nautilus multi-exercise machine.
Alternate compound exercises: High pulls with barbell, barbell cleans.

Delts:	1. Dumbbell laterals	
	2. Press behind neck	2 cycles
	3. Bent-over dumbbell laterals	2 sets

Alternate isolation exercises: Any type of curl.
Alternate compound exercise: Palms-up pulldown on lat machine.

POINTS TO KEEP IN MIND

1. There should be "zero rest time" between the first and second exercises of a cycle.
2. Strive to cut down on workout time, but don't rush so much that you compromise your workout efficiency.
3. Initiate all movements in a slow, deliberate fashion with no sudden jerk to get the weight moving.
4. Proceed through the range of motion, from full extension to full contraction and back again, in a deliberate fashion.
5. Your workouts should be progressive. Increase your weights whenever possible, but don't sacrifice proper technique. When a

weight that initially allowed six strict reps allows nine, increase the weight by 10 percent.

6. Fight the tendency to add more sets to the suggested workouts. Don't think you can make up for performing sets haphazardly by doing more haphazard sets. Doing more is rarely the answer to stimulating growth; harder is the answer, and the harder you train the less time you'll be capable of training.

7. You can change exercises whenever you wish—even every work-out. The important thing is that you adhere to the underlying principles.

8. Don't include the forced reps and negative resistance for each body part every workout. Going to total failure once a week for each body part is sufficient.

9. Never train more than four days a week. In many cases three days a week will be enough. Enough time must be allowed to elapse between workouts for recovery and growth.

10. This workout is not a guarantee of a Mr. America physique. It will allow you to gain only as rapidly as dictated by the limits of your genetic potential.

11. Don't begin this workout unless you've been training for at least one year on a regular basis.

12. If you work out on a three-day-a-week schedule, train on Monday, Wednesday, and Friday. Initially perform only one cycle if two are suggested and only one set if two sets are suggested. Increase the cycles and sets to two when you feel up to it.

13. If you find you are fatigued on a four-day-a-week schedule and see little progress, switch to a reduced frequency of workouts. Try training four days out of nine.

14. The tendency to add more sets and cycles will be natural, but always aim at training harder, not longer. As you advance, the likelihood of overtraining increases. Beginners are really too weak to overtrain. The larger and stronger muscles of the intermediate and advanced body-builders create much more intensity and place greater demands on the body.

15. Remember to perform negatives only once a week for any given exercise, for they raise the intensity dramatically and also increase the chances of overtraining.

16. Stay with this program for at least one year. If you are still making satisfying progress after a year, stay with it indefinitely. In most cases it will take two years to reach an advanced status.

·||| Chapter 28 |||·

HEAVY-DUTY
BODY-BUILDING

As the aspiring body-builder continues to progress, the muscles take on a full and rounded appearance. The formula for continued progress now becomes much more complex because of the changes in the body that attend such growth. The larger the muscles grow, the greater the demand imposed on the body's resources and reserves during intense muscular contractions. Physiologists have discovered that the average person has the capacity to increase strength and the ability to generate intensity by some 300 percent while the ability to recover from intense training stress increases by only 50 percent. So as we grow markedly larger and stronger even greater training intensity is required. This forces a reduction in training time to prevent the problem of overtraining. I found that after a number of years of forced reps and pre-exhaustion training, my progress became almost imperceptible. The problem centered around the fact that I was so strong, and my ability and willingness to generate maximum efforts so dramatically increased, each rep of a normal six- to eight-rep set was severe enough and the oxygen debt and lactic acid buildup were severe enough from the first rep that I was literally prevented from performing the maximum-intensity rep at the finish.

REST-PAUSE TRAINING

To circumvent these limiting factors I devised a program that provided for maximum-intensity contractions while at the same time slowing the rate at which metabolic waste products formed. The method I used is referred to as "rest-pause" training.

With rest-pause I warm up the given area thoroughly by performing a few lighter sets and then selecting a weight for the first rep of a set that is maximum for a single attempt. This, of course, ensures maximum intensity of effort. After the first all-out rep, I put the weight down and rest for ten seconds, long enough for oxygen to enter the muscles and for waste products to leave. This allows the second rep with the same weight to be all-out, maximum intensity. You will need a partner for rest-pause, as you may not be able to complete a second rep without just enough assistance to complete it. After the second rep, rest for ten seconds and reduce the weight by 20 percent so you can again do a complete rep by yourself. Perform a deliberate, controlled, all-out rep with the reduced weight. Rest up to fifteen seconds before the fourth rep and do it with assistance. Don't try to do more than four or five reps because it is very intense and demanding. With rest-pause every rep is maximum, not just the final rep, as with other, more conventional methods. This is why rest-pause is so different and superior. I also would recommend no more than one set per exercise for the same reason, and don't try more than three sets per body part. You can incorporate rest-pause into your normal routine. For example, when training the chest, do one set of incline presses rest-pause style, and proceed with one or two cycles of pre-exhaustion exercises. If you use rest-pause exclusively, don't continue for more than six weeks without switching back to more conventional exercises. It is as demanding mentally as it is physically, and it can cause "burnout" quickly.

TIPS FOR THE ADVANCED BODY-BUILDER

Now that you've been training for up to two years and have reached advanced status, you will need to perform increasingly intense workouts. Having developed so much muscle mass and strength, however, you will have difficulty finding appropriate routines. Rest-pause training will allow advanced body-builders to go beyond plateaus in progress, and beyond normal levels of intensity. Because rest-pause is so intense, the chances of overtraining are even greater than before.It's up to you to discover how many workouts a week you can employ.

1. If you want to continue with the same program as intermediates, you can increase the intensity by performing more negative training.

The amount of forced reps is up to you, since everyone has different needs and training intensity requirements.

2. No matter what routine you follow, always perform your exercises deliberately and under control. Don't ever try to yank, jerk, or bounce heavy weights. You'll never injure yourself if you "lift" heavy weights.

3. In all your exercises emphasize the negative or lowering of the weights. Exercise physiologists have discovered that in addition to preventing injury, performing exercises in this fashion raises the intensity of the workout. However, if you decide to use negative style only, break into it gradually, since lowering of the weight is primarily responsible for muscle soreness. If you aren't careful, crippling soreness can result.

4. Because of the greater intensity of your workouts, even fewer sets per body part are required. When performing purely rest-pause training, never do more than three sets per body part, and if mixing it with more conventional training such as pre-exhaustion or forced reps, never more than five sets per body part.

5. Under no circumstances should you train more than four days per week. Sufficient time is required between workouts for recovery as well as growth. Keep in mind that if you don't allow enough time for recovery, growth never will occur.

DIET

While it's true that increased levels of physical activity lead to faster fat losses, weight training is not the best way to drop fat. Workouts with weights should be used only for the purpose of maintaining or increasing muscle mass. The demands for energy imposed by anaerobic activities such as weight training are so great and immediate that adequate amounts of oxygen cannot be supplied rapidly enough to the muscles to metabolize fat for the required energy. Only glycogen, or the sugar stored within the muscle, can be metabolized in the absence of oxygen used as fuel for such anaerobic weight training.

When too few carbohydrates are included in the diet, the body cannot produce adequate quantities of glycogen, and the muscle itself can be broken down and sent to the liver, where it is transformed into glycogen and then used for intense muscular contraction. Only aerobic activities—those low-intensity, highly repetitive activities such as jogging, biking, or swimming—can use oxygen to burn stored fat, and they should be used regularly to help reduce body fat and increase definition.

The proper training formula in preparing for a contest should include weight-training sessions that progressively decline in intensity leading up to the contest, and aerobic activity that increases in duration and frequency before the contest. At the outset of any six- to ten-week contest preparation period, energy levels are bound to be higher, and the building of more muscle might still be a concern; hence training intensity is apt to be extremely high. With each week energy levels will probably drop somewhat due to the negative caloric balance and the increasing frequency and duration of other energy-consuming activities such as aerobics and posing practice. You should not be overly concerned with this inevitable decline in training intensity unless a marked decrease in strength and muscle size is noted as well.

If this happens, a re-examination of training activities and diet is necessary. Either you're grossly overtraining, or eating too few calories and carbohydrates, or both. Make the proper adjustments by cutting back on training duration and increasing caloric intake sensibly.

Maintaining adequate energy levels is imperative in the ongoing process of altering body composition. For a while the loss of body fat will be steady and will require little additional activity. Merely reducing caloric intake to a level below maintenance needs will result in fat loss. After a period, however, the body adjusts to the decreased caloric intake by burning calories at a slower rate in order to protect itself and to preserve body fat. This process is known as "adaptation to starvation." At that point a further reduction in caloric intake or greater caloric expenditure will be necessary. Rather than continuously reducing caloric intake and risking loss of muscle and reduced energy levels, it is better to increase voluntary activity. Aerobics are best suited for this.

At the beginning of the contest preparation period, the weight-training sessions will be very intense, so aerobic activity should be of relatively short duration; bike rides of 6 to 10 miles, jogging 1.5 to 2 miles every third day or twice a week will be adequate. As the contest gets closer, fat burning becomes an increasing concern, and the intensity of the weight sessions will decrease and the frequency and duration of aerobic activity should increase. Increase aerobic activity until you are biking at least twice a week for up to 30 minutes and running 3 to 5 miles twice a week. The biking and jogging balance is up to the individual, though biking can be done for a longer period and there is less strain on the joints. Running saves time in that it burns calories more quickly. A mile run burns 100 to 120 calories (15 calories a minute), while hiking at a moderate pace—8 to 13 miles per hour—burns only about 8 calories per minute.

Whichever activity you choose should be performed at a relaxed pace. If you are breathless, you are increasing the proportion of glucose being used as fuel and decreasing the use of fat as fuel. As body fat levels get lower, approaching the 3 to 6 percent level, the body will become increasingly alarmed and begin to preserve fat by releasing more sugar and muscle tissue for energy. A certain level of body fat is necessary for survival, and the body will alter its metabolism to preserve it.

To reach contest condition it is important to approach aerobic activities at a "conversational pace"; if you can't talk easily while jogging or biking, you are working too intensely. Reduce your pace, enjoy yourself, and burn fat at the same time.

Reducing your intake five hundred calories below maintenance and increasing normal activity to burn five hundred extra calories a day will use a thousand calories a day and result in a loss of about two pounds a week. While reducing calorie intake, strive to maintain a balanced diet that is comprised of 50 percent carbohydrates, 15 percent protein, and 35 percent fat. It's not recommended that you reduce daily intake to less than twelve hundred calories. Nutritional scientists have determined that it is difficult to get the necessary daily requirements of nutrients on such a low intake. Reducing calorie intake below this level is a risk to health and will inevitably result in some muscle loss.

A TRAINING JOURNAL

Experience will teach the competitor how to assess general condition and fat levels in order to map an appropriate diet and training regimen when preparing for a contest. There are so many factors to be considered and so many variables encountered over the course of a competitive career that it is difficult to retain all the knowledge gathered from experience. I doubt if there are any areas of human endeavor where a person discovers the most direct route from objective "A" to objective "B" at the outset. Learning and advancement are almost always reached through trial and error. By making a trial and missing the mark and then noting the error, you can make proper adjustments and move onward toward the goal. In order to develop your body to the maximum and learn how to reach a peak condition consistently, it is imperative that you avoid making the same mistakes twice.

If you view your training career as a journey whose destination is the fulfillment of your physical potential, a training journal will serve to map that journey. Keeping a record of every proper turn as well as every mistake can help you avoid the pitfalls and blind alleys which only slow you down.

A journal serves as a historical record of your diet and workouts and should include daily calorie intake (including the types of food), weights used in workouts, and sets and reps for all exercises. By recording and monitoring your daily food consumption, you can calculate your nutritional requirements for future weight gains and losses as well as observe the effects of certain diets on moods, training drive, and progress. Experimenting with different weights, sets, and repetition schemes and charting your progress will yield invaluable training data. Eventually you will have enough information in your journal to make precise determinations regarding dietary needs and training requirements. My own journal is kept in a hard-cover book, the kind that can be purchased in any stationery store. In it I keep a daily record of my weight, the foods I eat, their caloric content, the amount of weight for each exercise, and sets and reps. Before a contest I'll make detailed observations of my appearance. I record all other physical activities such as running and bicycling and the amount of time I spend practicing my posing. After each competition I go over the journal, making a careful analysis of everything I did in order to make necessary changes for the next competition.

·||| Chapter 29 |||·

POSING AND
PRESENTATION

If you hope to do as well as possible in physique competition, you have to
do your homework in the gym and pay strict attention to diet. But unless
adequate time and energy are devoted to posing and presentation, you
probably won't do well in the final judging. It isn't unusual to see lesser
physiques win over superior bodies because of polished stage performance.

Everyone possesses a unique assemblage of physical attributes in
addition to an individual personality and temperament. A posing routine,
to be effective, must complement your physical attributes and at the same
time express the essence of your personality. The style of posing you adopt
will serve as a complete expression of you. In selecting your poses, first
assess your physical structure. A person with a short, stocky physique
similar to that of a diminutive Hercules—Franco Columbu, for example—
would be foolhardy to attempt the ethereal, open-armed poses of the more
lithe Frank Zane.

It's up to the individual to select his or her poses from the
innumerable variety available to the imagination. A full repertoire should
include shots from all basic views—front, back, left side, right side. If you
neglect presenting your body from any one of these angles, the judges will
automatically assume you are hiding a weak point. After the basics,
include the more exotic kneeling, striding, and twisting poses. Limit
yourself, however, to no more than fifteen poses. Any more will be boring
and probably redundant. Incorporate them into a routine that allows for a

fluid and graceful transition from one pose to the next. Posing and presenting your physique properly requires considerable skill and represents the sporting side of body-building. But posing also requires that you express your individuality, which involves a certain amount of creativity and reflects the artistry in body-building.

As a so-called sport or art, free-style posing in body-building demands the mastery of technical skills along with artistic renditions. To the degree that posing expresses the feeling of the individual about himself and his relationship to the audience, it is a form of nonverbal communication. It's necessary to make each pose technically perfect, and this involves the proper placement of hands, feet, and head. You also need the ability simultaneously to flex every muscle that is being observed and display the appropriate facial expression.

As an art, posing is still evolving, and there is infinite room for creativity. It is obvious from watching the more accomplished body-builders, however, that effective posing should appear effortless, relaxed, graceful, and enjoyable for the poser. The transitions between each pose must be free-flowing, with all body parts moving uniformly and in a coordinated way. Most important, these transitions must contain elements of individual personality.

Infusing a posing routine with personality will require a great deal of practice and experience. It can't be taught.

Nevertheless, here are a few suggestions that will help you master the technical and artistic details of posing:

1. When practicing, it is important to relax and focus your thoughts on the task at hand; select an environment that is quiet and free of outside distractions.
2. Set aside at least three half-hour periods a week for posing practice. As a contest nears, increase the frequency of your posing practice sessions. In the last week you can drastically decrease the frequency of the workouts, even stop training entirely, and substitute daily or twice-daily posing sessions. (Muscle contractions during posing are intense enough to substitute for workouts.) Don't perform *any* vigorous activity the last day or two before a show. Relax, recuperate, and conserve your energy. Your routine must come as second nature, so practice, practice, practice. Nothing looks worse than a body-builder who forgets some part of his posing routine.
3. Get comfortable with the mirror. While body-builders often have been accused of being "mirror" athletes, I have observed just the opposite. Most body-builders are actually mirror-shy. Other than

the frequent spot check when the body-builder uses the mirror to monitor his or her appearance, much as the runner uses the stopwatch to monitor progress, few body-builders spend enough time in front of the mirror. Practicing the technical aspects of posing and analyzing the details of his appearance are extremely important. The mirror-shy body-builder must learn to relax in front of the mirror. It's the only way to improve posing. The best mirrors are the full-length, two- or three-angle variety. It also will help to practice under an overhead light that will illuminate you like stage lights.

4. Posing in front of a mirror can be a great aid, but don't limit your practice to the mirror. On a regular basis, have a friend familiar with body-building competition watch your routine and offer constructive and critical comments. This will help you correct any mistakes you may have overlooked while practicing alone.

5. If possible, have a competent photographer shoot stills or even movies of your routine. This will enable you to become a detached critic of your own posing. Photos taken during competition also will provide material for analysis and further upgrading of your appearance and routine.

6. Experiment and alter your posing routines from contest to contest. As your physique and competitive nature continue to evolve, so will your posing. Years of practice, experience, and experimentation are necessary before you can hope to express yourself fully and maturely through posing.

7. Since posing is a form of nonverbal communication, you must learn to talk to the audience with your body. Your body language onstage will affect the judges and audience on both conscious and unconscious levels. The very moment you appear onstage you begin conveying impressions to everyone. By being aware of this fact, you can control what you communicate. In addition to displaying your physical assets, it's important to exhibit a confident stage presence. Any expression of nervousness, uncertainty, or self-consciousness will cause you to appear weak and will affect the judges' decisions. The audience is very sensitive and will pick up any negative emotions. If you are in your best possible shape and have done your posing homework, you should walk onstage proud, confident, and happy. These feelings will be expressed naturally in your posing, which will be effectively topped with a heartfelt smile as you make your exit.

8. Equally as important as your posing and presentation is your overall appearance. Judging a physique is akin to judging a Thoroughbred horse. Nothing escapes scrutiny. Things such as skin texture,

grooming, attire, posture, and even your teeth paint a positive picture. Give yourself at least four to six weeks to work on a suntan. This will be enough time to develop a rich, even color rather than the red, blotchy appearance that a rush job or a sun lamp can create. If sunning is impossible, then use a suntan parlor.

9. Take good care of your skin as well. After your workouts, shower with warm water and soap. If you have a problem with blemishes, see a dermatologist. Get a haircut to suit your head and physique. Too much hair will enlarge the head and detract from your shoulder width. A trim, athletic cut is best.

10. Either buy an appropriately cut pair of posing trunks or have them custom made. If you have a long torso, your trunks should be relatively high on the waist. If you are short, then your trunks should be cut lower to create a more elongated appearance. If your thighs are short, your trunks should be cut higher; for longer legs, your trunks should be cut lower. If you enter the show with a deep, bronze skin tone, then the color of your trunks can range from a pale yellow to a hotter color like red. Lighter skins require earth tones like brown and green and should avoid flashy colors.

11. In addition to being well groomed, the condition of the face is extremely important. Moustaches may enhance certain facial types, but beards almost always detract. Be discriminating in either case. Take good care of your teeth, brushing after each meal and avoiding refined sugars in your diet. If your teeth are less than pearly white, have them professionally cleaned.

NUTRITION FOR CONTEST PREPARATION

Every body-builder should strive to gain muscle tissue without gaining fat. Occasionally, however, a small amount of fat may accumulate as a result of a small but undetected increase in calorie consumption. Even in those cases where scrupulous attention to diet has prevented fat buildup, it will probably be necessary to lose at least a few pounds in preparation for competition. Very few body-builders can, or should, maintain minimum body fat levels for an extended period.

In assessing your condition at the beginning of a contest preparation period, it's important to allow yourself enough time to lose as much fat as you can in the allotted six- to ten-week period. As I said, it's almost physiologically impossible to lose more than three pounds of fat a week, and it is safer to lose more slowly than that, to reduce the risk of burning up muscle tissue. Two pounds a week would better serve the competitor's aims. To lose two pounds a week you have to balance calorie intake with expenditure so the body burns seven thousand extra calories every seven days.

WINNING AND SPORTSMANSHIP

The commonly held belief that participation in athletics strengthens and broadens the character has come under increasing fire. As the case is now, the athletic ideal seems to emphasize certain traits at the expense of others—namely, aggression, competitiveness, and winning. As a competitor, I am the first to admit that the joys of competition are best capped by winning. A competitor who places too much emphasis on these traits, however, tends to neglect the more humanistic, subjective, and cooperative side. This imbalance in personality does not serve the individual or society at large because it alienates the athlete from a portion of himself and society.

Body-building competition can be fun and rewarding but only when it is placed in its proper perspective. Success does not really depend on winning or losing. If you look to the extrinsic rewards that usually come with winning a contest—fame, a trophy, money—to buttress your self-esteem or provide some long-term meaning for your life, you'll forever be snatching at crumbs. Expecting too much from such transitory benefits will lead inevitably to frustration and unhappiness.

As your competitive experience grows, outside motivation should give way to more lasting and meaningful intrinsic rewards. Winning or losing will become secondary in the pursuit of excellence. The happy and fulfilled body-builder will be the one who discovers that improved performance and inner confidence are what make competition a meaningful, joyous experience.

·||| Chapter 30 |||·

OLYMPIC WEIGHT LIFTING

Men have been lifting weights for centuries, most often out of necessity, but even as far back as the ancient Greeks there has been some form of competitive weight lifting. The name Mentzer originated in an area of Germany where people were known for centuries for their physical strength and their prowess in lifting heavy objects.

It wasn't until the invention of the dumbbell and the barbell in the 1800s that any sort of formal, regulated competitions took place. Today there are two types of competitive lifting. One is called Olympic lifting or just weight lifting, and consists of two lifts, the snatch, and the clean and jerk. The other is called power lifting, in which competitors perform three lifts—the bench press, the squat, and the dead lift.

Olympic lifting has been part of the games since the games in Athens in 1896, but there was little interest in the sport in the United States until after World War I. It wasn't until the 1932 Olympic games that the United States was represented by a full team in the eight weight classes used at that time.

After World War I, interest in weight lifting grew, largely because of a visit to America by Henry Steinborn, a German who was a strength expert and a professional wrestler of some note. Steinborn was an advocate of the "quick" lifts—the clean and jerk with one hand or two hands, the snatch with one hand or two hands, and the military press. He immediately gained a following and his instruction in these international lifting techniques was instrumental in getting the sport off the ground in this country.

The first official American meet using these lifts was held in 1924 at the York Barbell Club in York, Pennsylvania. In those early days, heavyweights who could clean and jerk 200 pounds were considered phenomenal. Today the world record in the 114.5-pound class is more than 300 pounds.

But more than records, these early meets stimulated interest in the sport and established York as the mecca of American weight lifting. In fact, it's quite possible that without the interest of Bob Hoffman and the people at York, Americans never would have risen to prominence in Olympic lifting.

In 1927 the first truly national competition was held and in 1929 the Amateur Athletic Union became the official sanctioning body for all weight-lifting meets. The AAU held the American championships in 1929 and in that meet the heavyweight champion snatched 203 and cleaned 286. The 1932 Olympics in Los Angeles was the first international showcase for an American team, and though they had only one third-place finish, they gained valuable experience and recognition.

The 1936 Olympic team included the legendary Tony Terlazzo, John Terpak, Walter and Bill Good, John Terry, and John Grimek, whose exploits in weight lifting and body-building are without equal. Terlazzo was the hero of that team, becoming the first American Olympic winner in weight lifting, but Terry also won a medal and took his place alongside Jesse Owens as one of the black stars of the games.

The United States continued to do quite well until the World Championships in Stockholm in 1953. The Soviets won that meet and thus served notice that they were a force to be reckoned with in the weight-lifting world. And by the time the 1964 Olympic games rolled around, the Soviet Union, Poland, Czechoslovakia, Hungary, and Romania had begun to dominate. That situation has remained relatively unchanged for almost twenty years. At the end of 1979, the Bulgarians and the Soviets held world records in ten of the eleven weight classes that are now contested, and records have continued to rise in a steady progression.

My introduction to the world of weight lifting occurred not long after I began body-building. My father, seeing that my training was not just a passing fancy, thought it might be a good idea if I had some expert guidance. He had two friends who filled the bill nicely. One was John Meyers, a bulky, heavily muscled power lifter, who had been training for many years, and the other was Russell Herzog, an Olympic lifter who trained with Meyers in an old garage just a few blocks from my house in Ephrata.

Seeing my genuine interest, the two men took me in and gave me some much-needed instruction, inspiration, and encouragement. In the next few months they taught me the rudiments of productive exercise and the fine points of proper lifting. Herzog was a master of the three Olympic lifts used then—the press, the snatch, and the clean and jerk—and had won several state titles. Under his influence I naturally gravitated to his style of lifting.

In the summer it was boiling and in the winter it was freezing, but we never missed a workout. I vividly recall doing squats in the cold garage in the dead of winter and having my nostrils freeze shut because of the cold. But it was worth it. I loved the exhilaration and the camaraderie and I also learned a lot.

I trained hard on the Olympic lifts during that period, but it wasn't all work and no play. At least once a month the three of us would make the thirty-mile trip to York, the mecca of weight lifting. People used to travel from all over the country to watch the famous lifters work out in the York gym.

Meyers, Herzog, and I sat among the pilgrims and I watched with awe and admiration as the powerful competitors lifted incredible poundages.

In particular, I remember watching Tony Garcey, Olympic and American champion in the 165-pound class, spend hours perfecting his technique in the snatch, a lift that requires tremendous coordination and motor skills. My favorite at the time was Bill March, also an Olympic and American champion, in the 198-pound class. I favored him because he was the most powerfully built man I had ever seen, and that's still true. He didn't train specifically as a body-builder but he had many of the natural physical attributes of a top body-building champion. He had broad shoulders and narrow hips and huge trapezius muscles that seemed to grow out of his ears and spread across his upper back. His spinal erectors were so large it was said he could crush an orange between them. The erectors and the trapezius are important to the Olympic lifter for pulling the weight from the floor and straightening up. March, who was also something of a showman, used his muscular development to win many physique titles as well. I still remember his act when there was a large crowd on hand. He would do a standing backflip and land on his feet, which is incredible considering he weighed 220 pounds and had thirty-inch thighs.

March's physique taught me the importance of performing heavy, basic lifts like the power clean and dead lift to develop density and thickness in the back muscles. Many body-builders make the mistake of training only the more showy latissimus muscles and never developing the density that comes from the spinal erectors.

John Grimek, now in his seventies, also used to show up in the York gym from time to time and would go through a light workout for the assembled fans. In addition to competing in Olympic lifting competitions, Grimek set records in power lifting, won the Mr. America title twice (the only man ever to do it), and was an accomplished acrobat. Grimek was named Mr. Universe at age forty, and when he received his trophy, he did a backflip and landed in the split position to the amazement and delight of the audience. Dr. John Ziegler, pioneer in the world of sports medicine, developer of anabolic steroids, and the York team physician, says "Janko," as he called Grimek, was quite possibly the greatest athlete of all time and without doubt the greatest all-around strength athlete who ever lived.

March and Grimek and many other weight lifters also had fine physiques. Tommy Kono, America's greatest lifter in the 1950s, once held records in four weight classes, yet he also won the Mr. Universe title. Sergio Oliva, a Mr. Universe and three-time Mr. Olympia, was a world-class weight lifter for Cuba before coming to the United States in the 1960s. Oliva settled in Chicago and teamed up with Bob Gajda, another former Mr. America and now a professor of biomechanics. Gajda saw Oliva's inherent body-building potential and helped turn him into a body-builder. At the same time, Gajda changed from body-building to weight lifting.

These examples of men who excelled in both body-building and weight lifting might make it seem that anyone can do it. But these are all rare individuals, born with just the right combination of genetic traits that enabled them to develop in both sports. Even in these cases the athlete usually opted for the sport in which he was more genetically qualified and ultimately gained greater success.

As with power lifting, physical size is not a limitation for those who want to become competitive Olympic lifters. Weight classes range from featherweight at 114.5 pounds, through superheavyweight, 242.5 pounds and over. During the 1950s and 1960s when I was making my visits to the York club, American lifting was in its heyday. Men like Ike Berger in the 132-pound class, Kono in four classes, Garcey at 165, March at 198, Norbert Shemanski and later Bob Benarski in the heavies, all helped make this country a world power in Olympic lifting.

Today Bulgaria, the Soviet Union, and East Germany rule the

Olympic lifting world, and it looks as if this will be the case for years to come. Olympic lifting is a major sport in most European countries and it attracts many potential standouts. In this country, the interest simply isn't there, so many athletes with lifting ability gravitate to other sports.

THE OLYMPIC LIFTS

There are ten weight classes, running from 114.5 pounds to 242.5 pounds and over. In official meets only ten competitors per country are permitted, with three reserves. No more than two lifters are permitted in any one weight class.

The Two-hand Snatch

The bar is placed on the floor in front of the lifter. The bar is gripped palms down, and pulled in a single movement from the floor to the full arms-extended position vertically above the head. The legs can either be split or bent. The bar must move continuously to the top and be held in the final position with the feet in the same line as the body. The bar must be held motionless until the referee gives the signal to return the bar to the platform.

The Two-hand Clean and Jerk

In the clean portion of the lift the bar is brought in a single movement from the floor to the shoulders. The legs may be split or bent. With the bar resting on the clavicles, the feet in a straight line with the body, the lifter is ready for the jerk.

In the jerk the bar is pressed to the full stretch of the arms over the head. The knees may be bent but they must be brought back into a straight line with the body. When the weight is motionless, the referee signals and it is returned to the floor.

The final score is determined by adding the total weight of both lifts. In case of a tie in any weight category, the lighter man wins. The lifter gets three tries at each weight.

·ǁǁ Chapter 31 ǁǁ·

POWER LIFTING

Power lifting is such a young sport that I clearly remember attending the first world championships in York, Pennsylvania, in 1965. Competitors were few, spectators sparse, and records minuscule compared to the extraordinary poundages lifted today. Still, I was duly impressed when Terry Todd, weighing over 300 pounds, squatted 600 pounds in the heavyweight class. Today, just sixteen years later, Mike Bridges, at 165 pounds, is squatting more than 750 pounds. And Jan Todd, one of the world's premier women lifters and Terry Todd's wife, squats well over 500 pounds. The same increases are occurring in the other two power lifts—the bench press and the dead lift.

Power lifting may be young as an organized sport (the International Power Lifting Federation wasn't formed until 1972, and the first women's championships weren't held until 1978), but it seems destined for rapid growth. There are at least two reasons for this. First, the three lifts require brief, explosive muscular efforts and some measure of coordination and agility, but they are quite simple to perform and take a much lower level of neuromuscular skill than the Olympic lifts. And second, the sport has quickly become popular with women, who can rapidly develop the strength and skill necessary to compete.

Television has also discovered power lifting, and champs like Mike Bridges, Bill Kazmaier, and Larry Pacifico have performed in front of international audiences numbering millions of people. The number of new participants and the heightened interest in weight lifting by athletes in all sports have led to advances in training methodology, and these in turn have resulted in the geometric leaps in power-lifting records.

In the past fifteen years or so, I've spent considerable training time practicing the power lifts because they are highly effective exercises for building muscular mass. Power lifters probably have the most massive musculature of all athletes, and every top body-builder, from Grimek, Reg Park, and Bill Pearl down to the present crop, has to give credit to power lifting for building the foundation of heavy muscle that is so important in physique competitions.

The effectiveness of these lifts lies in the fact that they bring the major muscles into play simultaneously and they force the lifter to use heavy weights. Both factors stimulate muscle growth. Even today, power lifting figures into my regular training schedule, usually after the contest season is over. I use it to build additional mass. For me this isn't quite as important a phase of training as it used to be, but for the beginning or intermediate body-builder it is essential.

Genetics, as always, plays a major role in the development of top power lifters. Size alone isn't all that important. Body type, overall proportions, skeletal formation, and muscular efficiency all enter into the equation. From a strictly mechanical point of view, there are certain body proportions that are more suitable than others for the power lifts.

People with large, deep chests and relatively short upper arms are better suited for bench pressing because they have less distance to press the weight. Those with torsos that are short in relation to their legs have a mechanical advantage that is a plus in the squat. Long arms and short torsos are advantageous for the dead lift. It's not likely that a body exists that is perfect for any two of these lifts, but lifters usually excel in one lift or another because of their skeletal structure. Power lifters also must have bones and connecting ligaments that are strong enough to support the heavy weights they use. At an exhibition in Chicago not long ago I was "spotting" for Mike Bridges while he attempted a world-record 750-pound squat. As he hoisted the bar from the rack to his seemingly frail back, I couldn't help but wonder how his 165-pound body was going to support such a weight without his spine snapping in half. Of course, he completed the squat with power to spare and no injury whatever, and with his skeletal structure still intact.

Neuromuscular efficiency is the relationship between the nervous system and the muscles. The brain and the central nervous system activate the muscles required for each movement. People with high levels of neuromuscular efficiency are able to contract a large percentage of their muscular mass, giving them an advantage over other power lifters and other athletes. A recently conducted Canadian study revealed that neuromuscular efficiency varies widely among individuals. The majority of people are able to contract about 30 percent of any muscle group in an all-out maximum effort. A few people rate at 40 percent. Their muscles are no bigger than average; they merely have the innate ability to contract a greater percentage of their muscle fibers. At the lower end of the muscle curve there is the occasional 10 percent person, and at the high end an occasional 50 percent person. These cases are both rare. The 50 percent rating constitutes a genetic freak in the strength category and it is this level that makes for super power lifting.

If you are very strong for your size and possess a high level of neuromuscular efficiency, then power lifting may be your sport.

THE LIFTS

As in Olympic lifting there are ten weight categories in power lifting, and in competition, countries are allowed only ten team members, with two alternates. A competitor's score is the total of all three lifts.

The Squat

The squat is performed almost exactly as it's been described in Chapter 12. Of course, form is very strictly observed. The weight is taken on the shoulders from a rack, and the lifter must step back before beginning the squat. At the bottom of the movement the thighs must be below parallel, and there is no bouncing allowed. When the lifter stands with the weight, he or she must remain motionless and then, at the referee's signal, attempt to put the weight back on the rack.

The Bench Press

Two positions are allowed on the bench, but in both the back must be flat on the bench surface at all times. The weight is taken from the stand and lowered to the chest. The weight must be pressed up to the full extension of the arms until the elbows are locked. The bar must be held in that position for two seconds.

The Dead Lift

The bar is placed on the floor in front of the lifter. It can be gripped in any manner with both hands. It is then lifted with one continuous motion until the lifter is standing straight with shoulders back and knees locked. When the bar is motionless, the referee signals the completion of the lift.

·|‖| Chapter 32 |‖|·

A BRIEF HISTORY OF BODY-BUILDING

The history of weight training and body-building is poorly recorded, though there is evidence that indicates people have been lifting weights for thousands of years. The information about systematic athletic training with weights is equally scarce.

That said, I think it's safe to assume that mankind has had an interest in, and a fascination with, great physical strength and muscular development since before recorded history. Size and strength have always been dominant factors in some societies, with leaders often being the largest, strongest, and bravest in the group. It's likely that the largest cavemen and cavewomen were also looked to for leadership. Mythology, sculpture, and vase painting all emphasize size and strength in many cultures.

Some recent discoveries suggest that weighted objects of various kinds were used in China for heavy exercise as far back as 3600 B.C., and wall paintings in the tomb of Beni Hassan show men and women of the Egyptian Empire (3500 B.C.) exercising with weights made of stone, marble, and lead. Chinese tomb paintings around 500 B.C. also show the use of weights for physical training.

It's entirely possible that the ancient Greeks, known for the high premium they placed on training the body and the mind, developed the first organized approach to weight training. Many training activities were born of practical necessity, since victory in warfare depended more on

Eugene Sandow

physical superiority and endurance than on weaponry in those days, and these training activities were gradually improved and refined until they became relatively sophisticated by the second century A.D.

Legend has it that weight-training and progressive-resistance exercise became popular around 300 B.C., when a shepherd in Crotona, a man named Milo, performed his daily exercise by carrying a newborn calf on his back. Milo, it is said, continued to carry the calf every day until it grew into a full-sized cow, and thus created progressive resistance exercise—increasing the weight used for training as strength increases.

Milo's training methods seemed to have worked. He won the Pythian games seven times and the Olympic games six times. In fact, records from that era indicate athletes began training with weights months in advance of the games, and there are illustrations that show athletes lifting stone dumbbells and other weights specially fitted to their bodies. The Greeks were in all likelihood the first body-builders, as their appreciation of physical beauty paralleled their admiration for athletic excellence.

The sculpture of ancient Greece gives ample evidence of the Greeks' love of physical beauty. Phidias created statues that depicted men at the peak of physical development. Of all the Greek sculptors, he was unsurpassed in representing the ultimate perfection of the male form. Perhaps the most representative of his works is Apoxyomenos, a statue of a well-developed athlete drying himself after an exercise session.

Eugene Sandow   *Bernarr Macfadden*

The Romans shared the Greeks' appreciation for athletic perfor-mance and physical development. Nero was a supporter of gymnastics and other sports, but as the Roman Empire began to lose its sense of purpose and direction the value of physical exercise diminished.

For centuries after the Roman Empire collapsed, there is little information to indicate an interest in things physical, with a few exceptions. The Vikings glorified muscular strength, and they were formidable warriors who fought stripped to the waist, their torsos bathed in oil. Their tradition of strength was passed to their descendants who settled in the Scandinavian countries, and today strength sports are popular in that part of the world.

It wasn't until the Renaissance in the fifteenth century that the body is again found as the subject of appreciation. Michelangelo and Leonardo produced renderings of the human body that showed an appreciation of anatomy and muscular development. Leonardo especially focused on the muscles and he made illustrations of the mechanical contraction and extension of the muscles during work.

But it wasn't until the eighteenth century that interest in physical strength reappeared. Physical education became an integral part of university curricula and was designed for the overall development of the body. It was during this period and into the nineteenth century that new and more productive exercise apparatuses were developed by innovative physical-education teachers. Frederick Jahn of Germany was in the forefront of this movement. He developed a new series of exercises and organized the Turner Societies, gymnastic groups that found their way to the United States with German immigrants in the 1850s. These societies figure prominently in the physical-culture movement in America, a movement that was to take a great leap forward with the development of progressive resistance exercises.

Hard physical training of the type we know today is a relatively recent concept. Most training in the formative years of the physical-culture movement concentrated on the creation of muscular strength first and put the development of the body for aesthetic purposes second. David Webster, one of the foremost authorities on the history of weight training, credits this shift in emphasis to Louis Durlacher, who, Webster says, "was one professional strongman who had the vision and foresight to see body-building as an activity in its own right."

Durlacher, better known by his stage name, Attila, traveled widely in Europe, performing stunts that were unique at the time. Yet his fame in the strength world came not so much from his stage show as from his teaching of physical culture. He eventually became known as the "Professor" for his work with other physical culturists and important members of European nobility. Durlacher had a strong influence on the greatest strength athletes of the day, including Louis Cyr, Warren Lincoln Travis, Lionel Strongfort, Adolph Nordquest, and James Corbett.

Attila is credited with the invention of hollow, shot-loaded dumbbells, and Webster says the earliest photo he has seen of a man exercising with cables featured Attila. His greatest contribution, however, may have been the help and inspiration he gave to an aspiring professional strongman, Eugene Sandow.

Sandow was born Frederick Mueller in East Prussia in 1867, and he rose to fame, with the help of Attila, by winning a strength contest from Charles Sampson, then called "The World's Strongest Man." Following his victory, Sandow traveled the world giving exhibitions of his strength and physique.

It wasn't until the 1890s that Sandow was to make his real fame and fortune. In 1893 Florenz Ziegfeld saw Sandow performing on Broadway and signed him for the World's Columbian Exposition, at Chicago. Sandow was a very big hit, and Ziegfeld signed him to a long-term contract at fifteen hundred dollars a week. It was Sandow's heroic stature that reminded a whole generation of the physically attractive male body, and his performances stirred the imagination of young men everywhere. He is considered the seminal influence on modern-day body-building, with its emphasis on massive muscular development and definition.

In the early 1900s body-building received another boost, this time from a publisher and businessman named Bernarr Macfadden. Macfadden picked up on the Sandow craze and promoted his own quasireligious approach to physical development through a magazine called *Physical Culture*. He used the slogan, "Weakness Is a Crime, Don't Be a Criminal," and through his publication he conducted one of the first physique competitions held anywhere. In 1903 he selected regional winners from their photographs and chose the winner at a final event staged in Madison Square Garden, in New York City. The champion was declared "The Most Perfectly Developed Man in the World."

Physique contests became popular after that, and in 1921 a real star burst on the body-building scene. That year Macfadden's contest winner was Angelo Siciliano, who went on to become Charles Atlas, the man who made body-building big business. Atlas sold his "dynamic tension" course through magazine ads all over the world. The ads, still in print today, show a skinny young man getting sand kicked in his face by a beach bully. The weakling takes Atlas's strength course, which quickly builds him into a muscular giant who returns to beat up the bully and reclaim his girl. The dynamic tension course, based on isometrics, still sells seventy thousand copies a year worldwide. It was Atlas who brought about a quantum leap in body-building popularity.

But weight training for the sole purpose of building muscle found its greatest exponent in Alan Calvert. The physical culturists before Calvert were more interested in health, vitality, and virility. Calvert's interest was pure physical strength and development. After seeing Sandow in Chicago, Calvert started training with barbells he made himself and he later established the Milo Barbell Company. Calvert began publishing pamphlets on weight training as an alternative to Macfadden's health-oriented publications, and this eventually led to Calvert's own magazine, called *Strength*. Through *Strength,* Calvert generated tremendous interest in weight training in the United States, and he became the undisputed leader in the field during the first quarter of this century. He was active, along with Macfadden, in promoting body-building contests in the 1920s and early 1930s, and by the late 1930s such competitions were being held everywhere.

In those early days, there were few standards regulating physique contests. It wasn't unusual to see some contestants onstage in boxer shorts, briefs, or even jockstraps. Judging standards were uneven, and there was no generalized scoring system. Then in 1939, the AAU stepped in and sanctioned the first Mr. America contest, an event won by Roland Essmaker. It was the next year, 1940, when John Grimek won the title and body-building forged into the modern era.

It was Grimek, more than any other man of that period, who demonstrated the ultimate potential of the male physique. He went on to

A BRIEF HISTORY OF BODY-BUILDING

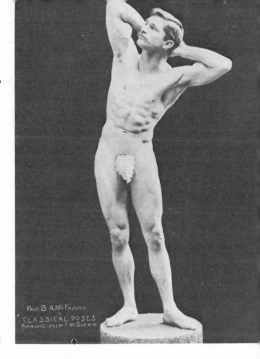

Bernarr Macfadden

win every major competition without once losing. Grimek's exploits inspired many young men to take up weight training. As a teenager I saw Grimek at many of the physique contests held in and around York, Pennsylvania. Although in his fifties at that time, the muscularity of his arms was still tremendously impressive and he still had broad shoulders and a small waist. Now in his early seventies, Grimek still trains three days a week and is in fine shape. He is also active as editor of *Muscular Development,* one of two magazines published by the York Barbell Company's founder and owner, Bob Hoffman.

Though Hoffman never won any physique titles or weight-lifting contest, he was a superior athlete and his contribution to modern weight lifting has been inestimable. Through the worldwide circulation of his magazines, Hoffman has spread the message of weight training and healthful living to countless millions. He has also lectured and written extensively about the value of weight lifting for athletes and in large measure is responsible for the widespread use of weights by today's athletes.

The AAU continues to sanction both weight lifting and physique competitions on local, state, and national levels, and in 1978 they affiliated with the International Federation of Body-builders. The IFBB was formed in 1946 by Joe and Ben Weider, and through their efforts, the organization has grown to 111 member countries, and it is the seventh-largest sports federation in the world. Much of the current popularity of body-building is due to the work of the Weiders.

Joe Weider's efforts since the mid-1940s have been channeled into his magazine *Muscle and Fitness,* which regularly publishes the training routines and diets of the top physique champions and the most recent information available from medical researchers. He has also spent considerable time and money training and promoting many champions, Mike Mentzer among them.

As body-building has grown in popularity, more attention has been paid to training practices which have produced men of much greater size and muscular definition. The prime example of this progress is Arnold Schwarzenegger, who won the Mr. Universe title five times and the Mr. Olympia contest, the Super Bowl of body-building, seven times. When Schwarzenegger was only nineteen he was brought to this country under the sponsorship of Joe Weider. Weider essentially paid Schwarzenegger to train, and he did, with a vengeance. His hard work and perseverance paid off in a body that has the biggest, most defined musculature any human being has yet achieved.

Schwarzenegger's success coincided with a growing public awareness of the need for exercise and proper nutrition, and as a result he became a personality, a leader in the physical-fitness movement. He proved to body-builders of my generation that the time was right to make a living at body-building.

John Grimek

A BRIEF HISTORY OF BODY-BUILDING

Bill Pearl

In the 1970s and now in the 1980s, a growing number of young, ambitious body-builders have turned professional. The IFBB has steadily added to the number of competitions held annually, and this has furthered the sport's development. When Schwarzenegger won his sixth Mr. Olympia contest in 1975 it was the only pro body-building contest that year, and he won the total prize money, one thousand dollars. The prize money for the Mr. Olympia contest has climbed every year and reached fifty thousand dollars in 1980, with twenty thousand dollars going to the winner. Total prize money for all the professional contests held in 1980 came to more than two hundred thousand dollars.

Body-building's growing acceptance has been aided by television coverage of many important contests, and in 1981 all three commercial networks televised major competitions. In light of the trend toward fitness, and the knowledge that strength is a major component of fitness, it appears that the future of weight training is bright indeed. No longer is it considered an esoteric activity practiced by some strange subculture. And as more research in this area verifies the many values of weight training, even more people will become devotees of this once badly misunderstood method of physical training.

BODY-BUILDING PUBLICATIONS

Until recently, it has been difficult to find accurate, scientifically sound sources of information on exercise and fitness. Despite this fact, or maybe because of it, health and physical-fitness publications have flourished. Since before the turn of the century, in this country and abroad, there have been scores of ventures aimed at the physical-culture market. Many of these have been merely faddish; others have been the work of a dedicated but not necessarily knowledgeable zealot; and still others have, almost accidentally, provided useful information for the serious trainer as well as the average person looking for a little guidance.

It was *The National Police Gazette* that led the way in this field. *The Gazette*, founded in 1846, ultimately reached a weekly circulation of more than two million in the 1890s, and it served as the prototype of today's sports magazines and sports sections in the newspapers. *The Gazette* was not a muscle magazine or even a sports magazine as we know these publications today, but it was the first publication to devote space to sports regularly. In addition, the publisher, Richard Fox, sponsored physical contests of all kinds, including strength competitions. The paper featured news and instructional material about physical fitness and wrote about sports personalities, especially boxers. And though its main focus was on crime, gossip, adventure, and scandal, *The Gazette* served as a model for the physical-culture magazines that came on the scene in the early 1900s.

The physical culturists were a new and unique breed of hardy and opinionated individualists best exemplified by Bernarr Macfadden. Macfadden was by far the best known of the early physical culturists and his popularity continued until his death in 1955 at the age of eighty-seven. Obviously a man who practiced what he preached, Macfadden was parachuting in his seventies. At one time, his publications, *Health and Strength*, first published in 1889, and his most popular magazine, *Physical Culture*, had a combined circulation of more than thirty million copies a year.

Macfadden wrote extensively on body-building and strength and he was a pioneer in the world of fitness, espousing views that were far ahead of their time. In a typical editorial written in 1901, he advocated the "annihilation of the horrible curses of humanity," which included "prudishness, corsets, muscular inactivity, gluttony, drugs, and alcohol."

Physical Culture fired the imagination of other fitness fanatics and spawned a group of imitators. In the 1920s, *Health and Life* extolled the virtues of exercise, balanced diet, and weight training, and in the 1930s, *Superman* billed itself as the national physical-culture monthly and featured weight lifting as the means of achieving physical perfection.

The physical culturists gradually gave way to the more contemporary health and fitness publications that began to appear in the mid-1930s. The York Barbell Company and Bob Hoffman founded *Strength and Health*, a monthly devoted to weight lifting, and *Muscular Development*, a

Joe and Ben Weider with Mr. America contestants, 1962

bimonthly aimed at body-builders. Both magazines are still published and have large audiences of dedicated followers. In Alliance, Nebraska, in the 1940s, Peary Rader began a bimonthly magazine called *Ironman*, which is still very popular with hard-core body-builders. This was followed by *Muscle Digest*, written by Dr. Donald Wong for power lifters, *Muscle Magazine International*, Robert Kennedy's body-building bimonthly from Canada, and *Muscle Training Illustrated*, a product of the Dan Lurie body-building equipment company.

Certainly many other weight-training and fitness magazines have come and gone in the past fifty years, most without leaving a trace of their existence. Today, the field is dominated by the two magazines from York and Joe Weider's *Muscle Builder and Power*, edited and published in Woodland Hills, California. Weider bills his monthly as the "official journal" of the International Federation of Body-building, and he claims a circulation of more than three hundred thousand. *Muscle* is a more sophisticated publication, containing personality profiles, training routines, and nutrition articles designed for the consumption of both men and women body-builders. Weider also sells his own equipment and health products in the same way that *Strength and Health* serves as an in-house advertising medium for York equipment and vitamins.

The rising popularity of weight training, body-building, and fitness in general will undoubtedly encourage new publishing ventures in the future, and in fact, Weider has a body-building magazine for women on the drawing board. *Shape* was scheduled for publication in late 1981.

Still, looking back over Macfadden's *Physical Culture*, it's hard to imagine anyone reaching the heights of creativity, advocacy, and the pure joy that he found in publicizing the positive qualities of a healthy mind and a healthy body.

INDEX